ROBERT SECOR and MARIE SECOR

The Return of the Good Soldier: Ford Madox Ford and Violet Hunt's 1917 Diary

English Literary Studies

University of Victoria

1983

ISBN 0-920604-13-7

The ELS Monograph Series is published in consultation with members of the Department by ENGLISH LITERARY STUDIES, Department of English, University of Victoria, B.C., Canada.

ELS Monograph Series No. 30
© 1983 by Robert Secor and Marie Secor

CONTENTS

ACKNOWLEDGMENTS

We are grateful to The Pennsylvania State University Libraries for permission to publish Violet Hunt's 1917 diary, which is in the Rare Book Room at Pattee Library. Grants from the Institute of the Arts and Humanistic Studies, administered by Professor Stanley Weintraub, and the Liberal Arts Research Office facilitated research in several other libraries. We thank Donald D. Eddy, Librarian, and the Department of Rare Books, Cornell University Library, for allowing us to make use of the Hunt diaries and various letters and unpublished papers in its Ford Collection. Unless otherwise identified, all illustrations are courtesy of Cornell University Library. We are grateful to the New York Public Library and the University of Virginia Library for allowing us to make use of their special collections. We thank Professor Leon Edel, who made unpublished letters of Henry James available to us, and Edward Naumberg, Jr., who kindly let us examine the Ford and Hunt material in his impressive private collection. Dame Rebecca West, Norah Hoult, and Renée Haynes generously shared their memories of Hunt and Ford with us. Professor James Rambeau gave our manuscript a careful reading. We thank Margie Melton for her patient typing of our transcription of the diary. We wish to acknowledge especially Professor Charles Mann, Rare Book Librarian at Pattee Library, for sharing his expertise, and Aparna Dharwadker, who supplied invaluable research assistance.

INTRODUCTION

I.   The Diary

Violet Hunt's 1917 diary deserves our attention for a number of reasons. First, simply as a story, a narrative whose events are causally linked, it is surprisingly coherent and complete. Of course, the diarist cannot claim the benefits of foresight or afterthought available to the autobiographer or memoirist, so it is fortuitous when a string of events bounded by the calendar turns out to have a shape. This year in Hunt's life did. In terms of events, it begins with the absence of Ford Madox Ford, with whom she had been living since 1910; it then depicts his return and the final disintegration of their relationship. In terms of Hunt's own story, it moves from her initial awareness of Ford's intent to leave her to her full absorption of the impact of this decision. In terms of Ford's biography, it offers a perspective on the waning of one relationship (Ford and Violet Hunt) and the waxing of another (Ford and Stella Bowen). And as a story, it contains two sharply defined characters: Ford—elusive, phlegmatic, and impenetrable, and Hunt—desperate, confused, shrewd, but self-destructive. The lives of many other literary and artistic figures who enter the pages of Hunt's diary provide a counterpoint to those of Ford and Hunt. In their comments and advice, Hunt's friends offer interpretation, evaluation, and prediction. Her diary, then, is not just a list of social engagements; it is a monodrama, complete with recalled dialogue and choral commentary.

Given Hunt's peculiar skills as a writer, we should not be surprised that this is so, since she was notable for her wit, her frankness, and her insight into the perverse dynamics of sexual intrigue. She was nothing if not a "clever" writer, and her own life, painful as it was, provided a most congenial subject for her verbal and dramatic gifts. In fiction and memoir she exercised her talents for autobiography in *Their Hearts, Their Lives, Sooner or Later*, and *The Flurried Years*, "telling all" about her relationships with family and lovers. The self-expressive diary was thus a congenial mode for such a personal writer.

In any good story, action takes place against a backdrop, both human and historical. Violet Hunt's diary is notable for its richness of social context. She was, throughout her adult life and even before that through

7

her mother's social activity, energetically social. "You *are* Society," said her good friend and frequent companion, Henry James, as he followed from Rye her frantic London life with awe and curiosity, "but not a shred of envy."[1] Her earliest diaries (1882) depict the almost dizzying rounds of tea, visits, dinners, and parties she participated in through her parents' circle; by 1917 the names of the visitors have changed, from Robert Browning and Oscar Wilde to Ezra Pound and Rebecca West, but the pace has not abated. Douglas Goldring, in his memoir of South Lodge, remembers Hunt (and Ford) always ready to host or attend a party no matter what the state of their personal relations, and she always tried to fill her house on Campden Hill with the brightest literary and artistic lights she could attract. The society of South Lodge, he recalled, "had few connections with the fox-hunting aristocracy and the naval, military, and diplomatic caste formed by its offshoots," but "it was probably the most amusing, the most intelligent and the most worthwhile that late Victorian London had to offer."[2] The strong Pre-Raphaelite influence from Hunt's youth carried over into the acceptance of the bohemian and the slightly radical, but Hunt's guests nevertheless "dressed for dinner." As the diary reveals, the people who pass through Hunt's life in 1917 constitute a varied group. Some are old family friends, like Mrs. Pitt Lewis and Edward Heron-Allen, relationships Hunt maintained over the years. Others are military associates of Ford, and a few are politically involved, like the Pauls and the Mastermans, though Hunt took little interest in politics in the abstract. The dominant presence is that of the eminent and near-eminent literary and artistic lights of the time—people like Ezra Pound, Rebecca West, H. G. Wells, May Sinclair, Ethel Colburn Mayne, W. L. George, Arthur Watts, Marguerite Hall, Clemence Dane, Edgar Jepson, René Byles, etc.

Many of the men with whom Hunt associated led bohemian lives or carried on irregular relationships (Somerset Maugham, Wells, Gilbert Frankau, W. L. George, Gilbert Cannan, Marc-André Raffalovitch), but they never suffered the social opprobrium that befell her and her more adventurous women friends like Marguerite Hall and Rebecca West. Hunt seems to have had conflicting impulses, to be drawn both to the socially and artistically adventurous and to the wholly conventional, respectable upper-middle class: she wanted to be shocking and to be respected. Of course the first precluded the second. As her social circle diminished in her later years, she was left without the support of family, friends, even of her literary associates—and to her that social support was all-important.

8

The historical setting of this diary also lends it interest for the modern reader. It offers us a glimpse of England at war through the eyes of one affected by the war, but one who did not cultivate political consciousness. The war for Hunt is certainly a powerful influence on her life in 1917, as she learns of Ford being promoted and demoted, being moved from one place to another by apparently arbitrary powers, being assigned to different kinds of duty for inscrutable reasons. Other people involved in the war also pass through her diary, counterpointing the story of her relationship with Ford. They include Colonel Powell and his wife, involved with Ford in amorous intrigue; the eccentric Captain Marno; Sextus Masterman, who carries stories of Ford's military activities; and the women who stay behind during the war. Some of those who remained behind, like Mrs. Pitt Lewis, worried about their sons, others were busily involved in war work, but all of them were inconvenienced in matters ranging from the availability of Paris fashions to the functioning of transit and communications systems and the availability of food.

The war influenced every aspect of life for those at home as well as those more directly involved in the fighting: pacifists got involved in angry altercations, both personal and public; Hunt endured the suspicion of her neighbors because of her association with Ford, who just before the war announced that he had reclaimed his German citizenship; and as the year wore on, the increasing frequency of the air raids seemed to unnerve everyone, as shrapnel fell from the air with random, casual deadliness. Although in a 1916 letter to Lucy Masterman, Ford had spoken of Hunt as being "absolutely untouched, mentally, by the war— wh. is no doubt a blessed state,"[3] this diary shows that being untouched intellectually did not mean that she was untouched emotionally. When at one point she put on Ford's tin helmet, tied it under her chin with a pink ribbon, and made a grand entrance at a party, Grace Crawford wondered whether she was seriously afraid or making a joke.[4] As we read her diary, we know the answer.

Hunt emerges from her diary as a woman caught between unreconcilable forces: her desire for respectability and her pursuit of amorous sensation; her shrewd insight into her own and Ford's character and her self-destructiveness in protracting a relationship she knows is doomed to failure; her self-dramatizing instinct, always ready to step back and watch herself in action, and her spontaneity, equally ready to blurt out intimacies with dangerous frankness; her pride and her abjectness; her weakness and her vigorous fighting spirit; her wit and her sadness. She was a woman ill-at-ease in her time, too daring for the upper-middle-class

9

society whose approbation she craved, too conventional at heart to be a free-spirited bohemian, too old, really, to take advantage of the new freedom that emerged after the war. With characteristic self-awareness, she admitted to being an old New Woman: in the twenties she described herself accurately as "Not the Newest Woman of all, but I happen to be the New Woman that people wrote about in the nineties."[5] The New Woman of the nineties was still scandalous in 1917, but among the changes wrought by the war was a still Newer Woman, whose ambitions went beyond suffrage and latch keys, and Hunt knew what the difference was: "Does post-war woman realize the differentiation of the standard of manners that has obtained since 1918? In pre-war days Hamlet's brutal suggestion to the debutante Ophelia was perfectly practical politics —'Be thou chaste as ice and cold as snow, thou shalt not 'scape calumny,' or accept male escort in any circumstances whatever."[6] Although Hunt was never exactly as "chaste as ice," she was well aware that behavior for which she was pilloried before the war went unchallenged after it and that many of her younger friends enjoyed a social and sexual freedom unavailable to her.

Ford, the other principal actor in the drama, is physically absent from South Lodge during much of 1917, but obsessively present in Hunt's thoughts. When he does appear, he is rendered as sharply as a character in one of his own best novels. We learn from Hunt's diary some new facts about Ford—his movements during the year, the Miss Ross episode, the gambling debt incident, the first meeting with Stella Bowen, the flirtation with Colonel Powell's wife, the conflicts with Hunt over money —and we even get snatches of his dialogue, as Hunt remembered and recorded it. But more than providing biographical data, her diary creates an impression of a character—not a complete and static portrait, but a sketch, an impression executed in a technique similar to Ford's own fictional method in *The Good Soldier* and the *Parade's End* novels. We observe Ford through the lens of an obsessive vision, magnified and perhaps distorted, but Hunt's consciousness was never so narrow as to give us a caricature, and her sketch does capture subtleties and suggest mysteries. The Ford depicted in Hunt's diary can certainly be judged harshly; he is cruel, elusive, often dishonest, sometimes self-deceived, maddeningly self-protective, deliberately obtuse. But he is also in distress as great as hers, shattered and confused by a war experience he could not assimilate and trapped in a relationship he could not escape cleanly. Ford's withdrawal seems defensive and as inevitable, given the pattern of their lives, as Hunt's relentless poking at the ruined fragments of their life together.

Hunt's diary is painful reading precisely because it gives us two characters, not one. Her sketch of Ford is hardly objective, not to speak of sympathetic, but it is the impression of a woman who was not wholly blinded by her own pain. She knew Ford was a changed man, beyond her reach, no matter how she strained after him.

Finally, to the extent that Hunt's diary offers portraits of Ford and herself, it also helps us to understand Ford's fiction. Of all novelists, Ford is one whose biography is reflected most fully in his fiction, not so much because his novels are directly autobiographical (for they are not), as because of his impressionistic technique, which bent and transformed the events of his life into the objective correlatives of fiction, retaining the emotional "feel" they had for him while breaking up their realistic surface into tiny glints of rendered experience. For this reason, to know Ford's fiction is to understand the emotional tenor of his life, and to know the details of his life is to grasp the components of his fiction. Thus Allen Tate called upon any biographer of Ford to "understand at the outset that Ford himself must be approached as a character in a novel, and that novel a novel by Ford. . . . So the biographer must collect and compare the views—as Dowell [the narrator of *The Good Soldier*] collects and compares—of Jessie Conrad and Violet Hunt, and . . . Mr. Douglas Goldring."[7]

Because Ford was such a magpie collector of impressions and experiences that he worked into the fabric of his own creations, many of the events described by Hunt in her 1917 diary will sound familiar to readers of Ford, especially of the *Parade's End* novels. In addition to confirming the large correspondences between Violet Hunt and Sylvia Tietjens, this diary reveals many details of resemblance between them. At several points in her diary, Hunt confesses her rage and her boredom (June 16, August 9), a boredom which explodes into incessant talk about Ford. Like Sylvia, she is "bored . . . bored . . . bored!" and "Forever talking: usually cleverly, with imbecility; with maddening inaccuracy, with wicked penetration, and clamouring to be contradicted." Just as Hunt speculates about Ford's patronage of whorehouses in Rouen and his escapade with the "garrison hack" Miss Ross, so also is Sylvia obsessed by her need "to find out whether he [Tietjens] has that girl in Rouen." Christopher Tietjens informs his brother Mark that "Sylvia delighted most in doing what she called pulling the strings of shower-baths. She did extravagant things, mostly of a cruel kind, for the fun of seeing what would happen." Similarly, when Hunt surprised Ford on September 9 by sending him a check to pay a gambling debt he denied incurring, she is aware that her action exposes Ford. "A showerbath string pulled," she writes. And just as Sylvia is goaded into violence by Tietjens' impermeability, at one point striking him in frustration, at another exclaiming "I swear I'll make his wooden face wince yet," so too does Hunt report that she actually pummeled Ford in her rage several times during 1917 (August 24 and October 24), hoping to break through his impassiveness. The many unpleasant bedroom scenes between Hunt and Ford show her like Sylvia expecting "to have the whole night in which luxuriously to torment the lump opposite her. To torment him and to allure him." Reading Violet Hunt's 1917 diary is like being thrust through to the dark side of a mirror; it is like re-entering the *Parade's End* novels from the point of view of Sylvia Tietjens.[8]

II.   The Context

When we place this diary in the context of the Ford-Hunt relationship, and the relationship itself in the context of the patterns of each of their lives, the love affair and the last moments of its disintegration caught by the diary appear almost inevitable. First, the pair were drawn together by their common background. Ford (born Hueffer) has been called "the last Pre-Raphaelite," and with even greater insistence Hunt considered herself a Pre-Raphaelite daughter. Her father, Alfred Hunt, was a landscape painter with Pre-Raphaelite tendencies. As such, he was championed by Ruskin, a close family friend and godfather of one of Violet's sisters.[9] Alfred knew all the Pre-Raphaelites and was particularly intimate with Ford's grandfather, Ford Madox Brown. As a young girl, Violet listened to the talk of the prominent artists and writers who came to her home, and with her father she visited the studios of his Pre-Raphaelite friends, recording her observations in her early diaries. While still in her teens, and with the Pre-Raphaelites as her models, she studied painting at the South Kensington Art School and began writing poetry and fiction. As late as 1931, when she contributed to an exhibition of author-artists at Foyle's Art Gallery, newspaper reviewers noted the Pre-Raphaelite influence on her work.[10] The families of Hunt and Ford thus moved in the same circles, and while Violet's eleven-year head start made her too old to be a childhood playmate, she did recall trying to control Ford and his brother at children's parties, when the two Hueffer boys started pelting each other with penny buns.

Thus when Hunt and Ford met again at the Galsworthys years later, in March of 1907, they strolled afterwards down the Kensington Road sharing Pre-Raphaelite memories. The following month, encountering Ford as she left her publisher's office, she asked him to pump her next novel, *White Rose of Weary Leaf*. "He was awfully amused at my brass," Hunt recorded in a diary, and a month later Ford accepted her invitation to a garden party at South Lodge. Then, on October 16, 1908, at the suggestion of her friend H. G. Wells, Hunt brought some of her stories to Ford for *The English Review*. He immediately selected one ("The Coach") for publication, and Hunt subsequently became part of *The English Review* crowd, serving the journal as reader, contributor, and occasional sub-editor. By May of 1909, Ford was telling her he was in love with her, and at the end of the month he joined her at her cottage at Selsey.

Of course, it was more than their Pre-Raphaelite memories that brought Hunt and Ford together. By the end of 1909, Ford's wife, Elsie Martindale Hueffer, was spending most of her time in Winchelsea, too ill for the London air and suspicious of Ford's new circle of city friends. For his part, Ford was convinced that his life now belonged on Campden Hill:

> Campden Hill, in the royal borough of Kensington, was like a high class Greenwich Village, in which all the artists should be wealthy, refined, delicate and well-born. It was high in the air. In its almost country roads you met ladies all of whom wore sable coats—or at least sable stoles; & admirable children all bursting with health; and Whistler and Abbey and Henry James.[11]

Violet Hunt, confidante of Henry James, was the most eligible of these fashionable ladies. In her home on Campden Hill, Ford found a welcome escape from the depressing offices of the now bankrupt *English Review* at 84 Holland Park Avenue. She offered Ford financial rescue as well. In later years, Hunt looked back cynically at the attraction she held for Ford, describing herself as "a woman at a loose end of life, with a visiting list of notabilities as long as your arm and some experience of literature."[12] Among these notables was the wealthy liberal politician, Sir Alfred Mond, who in 1909 Hunt induced to buy the *Review* in order to salvage it.

At the same time, there can be no question that Hunt satisfied Ford's emotional and physical needs during this difficult period. In his self-pity,

Ford felt lonely and misunderstood. "What he needed was sympathy and consolation; what he dreamed of was a grand passion into which he could fling himself at the same time that he was confounding his enemies by making a splendid success of the Review."[13] Again, Hunt seemed to be in the right place for Ford. "An adventuress of the emotions,"[14] as Margaret Drabble has called her, she offered Ford all the romance he could have wished for. And if he wanted sexual excitement, he would have been hard pressed to find a woman who pursued it with greater avidity. Hunt herself had speculated that her interests were "too purely sexual" for her friend Arnold Bennett, and she admitted that she enjoyed shocking Henry James.[15] At forty-six, Violet Hunt was no longer the Pre-Raphaelite beauty some had called her in her youth, but she was still attractive. Goldring, who met her about this time, described "her large, liquid eyes, slightly arched nose and petulent, discontented mouth, [which] contributed to a still exciting sex-appeal."[16] Perhaps D. H. Lawrence caught best the attitude Hunt struck with Ford when he met them several years later, in 1912. Lawrence himself was at the time a young man in his mid-twenties, and he was as much aware of Hunt's age as of her seductiveness:

> She looked old, yet she was gay—she was gay, she laughed, she bent and fluttered in the wind of joy. She coquetted and played beautifully with Hueffer: she loves him distractedly—she was charming, and I loved her. But my God, she looked old. . . .
> I think Fordy liked it—but was rather scared. He feels, poor fish, the hooks are through his gills this time—and they *are*. . . .[17]

For her part, Hunt had good reason to sink her hooks into this fish. If Ford was in a state of despair when she came into his life in 1908, Hunt was herself in a state of emotional distress, still smarting from an unhappy affair with Oswald Crawfurd, another editor and married man. And if Hunt's connections were the right ones for Ford, so in turn were his for Hunt, whose ambitions were literary as well as social. By the time of the Ford affair, she was well launched in literary England, not only as a contributor to such journals as *Black & White*, *Chapman's Magazine*, *The Venture*, and *The English Review*, but as a novelist of some merit and popularity. She had caused a stir when she treated her grand passion for Crawfurd in *Sooner or Later* in 1904, but her major success was the more recent *White Rose of Weary Leaf* in 1908. The novel, which concerned a Brontëish governess-heroine in a modern setting, sold well and got itself banned by Boots circulating library as inappropriate reading for girls. Hunt wrote to Boots objecting, somewhat disingenuously: "I am enclosing my photograph and I should like to ask if you think it looks like the authoress of an improper novel."[18]

Her achievement and promise as a writer at the time her affair with Ford was about to bloom are perhaps best revealed by the comments of her literary friends after reading *White Rose*. Wells wrote, "I think it altogether the most interesting book you've done and the most probable success. . . . If you go on you will be a credit to the Fabian Society." Galsworthy thanked her for writing the book, saying "your heroine is quite a creation, and you have let us into many workings of the woman's mind—not only through your characters but through yourself." May Sinclair was delighted with the power of the book: "It seems to me that you've done what Hardy only tried to do when he wrote Tess. It took a woman to do it!"[19] An author with such promise and ambitions could do worse than form an alliance with the editor of *The English Review* and enter his circle.

Ford's sexual appeal was not so blatant as Hunt's, but the record of his conquests suggests that he had his attractions. "O Father O'Ford, you've a masterful way with you / Maid, wife and widow are wild to make hay with you,"[20] teased Joyce in a bit of doggerel. Perhaps Stella Bowen articulated Ford's appeal best: "The stiff, rather alarming exterior, and the conventional omniscient manner, concealed a highly complicated emotional machinery. It produced an effect of tragic vulnerability; tragic because the scope of his understanding and the breadth of his imagination had produced a great edifice which was plainly in need of more support than was inherent in the structure itself. A walking temptation to any woman, had I but known it."[21] The appeal of Ford's tragic vulnerability, along with Hunt's sense that at forty-six she needed a lifeline even more than he did, made her succumb to the temptation.

The unpublished love letters between Ford and Hunt during the summer of 1909 suggest that, as Lawrence believed, this time the fish was really caught. Ford praised both her sympathetic imagination, which for him proved her a poet, and her poetry, which expressed the fierceness and tenderness that had saved his life and his reason. Ford claimed that he was not jealous of Hunt's memories, but rather that her experience had made her all the richer and a bit mysterious to him. Thirty years earlier, young Oscar Wilde had playfully promised the teen-aged Hunt, "We will rule the world—you and I—you with your looks and I with my wits."[22] Now Ford expresses a similar dream of conquest, saying that they will make "a goodly couple," beside whom such literary lights as Shaw and Galsworthy will appear but "slow-witted fools." It was easy for Ford to convince himself that Hunt's vitality made their eleven-year age difference irrelevant, since she was for him "the only live creature in the world!" Hunt's letters at this time are equally loving, but their intensity conveys a note of foreboding: "I love you so very desperately—and for ever— . . . I never thought there was anybody in the world like you for me." When she has a chance to have her hand read, she refuses, "because I am so afraid of *not* being told that I am 'going to be married!' Tu comprends! I am deadly afraid of knowing anything for certain, except that. . . ."[23]

Uncertain about their future, Ford and Hunt lived all the more intensely in the present. "Violet had something of the Elizabethan pirate in her," David Garnett says, "and refusing to keep quiet, organized rounds of social visits for them both as though bent on singeing Mrs Grundy's beard."[24] H. G. Wells wrote warningly to her, saying he feared she was getting into a mess. When in November of 1909 Henry James learned from Ford of the couple's hope that Elsie would sue for divorce, he expressed horror at the prospect of Hunt's exposing herself to public proceedings and to show his concern withdrew an invitation to Lamb House. "I deeply regret and deplore the lamentable position in which I gather you have put yourself," he wrote her. "It affects me as painfully unedifying, and compels me to regard all agreeable or unembarrassed communications between us as impossible. I can neither suffer you to come down to hear me utter those homely truths, nor pretend at such a time to free or natural discourse of other things on a basis of avoidance of what must be most to the front in your consciousness or what in a very unwelcome fashion disconcerts mine." Hunt responded that she was not at all in a "lamentable position," that Elsie could not name her as co-respondent because her relations with Ford were "chiefly editorial." Moreover, she assured her old friend, "I should have listened humbly enough to home truths from you, if only a certain amount of the sympathy on which I have learnt to count was behind it."[25]

There was, however, to be no petition from Ford's wife, for in the previous month Elsie had caught the couple with their luggage at the Charing Cross station. "I had been abroad, staying with respectable, God-fearing friends, chaperoned to the hilt, or the nines!" Hunt laments unconvincingly in her memoirs. "On the cynical face of it I appeared to be returning from a trip to the Continent with a married man."[26] Ford judged the situation correctly when, leaning over to Hunt, he muttered, "It's all up, old girl! You will see. There'll be no divorce." Indeed, Elsie's Catholic family, who had opposed the idea of divorce from the start, were now able to dissuade her from taking action. "Oh dear, if people had not stepped in," Elsie reflected years later. "Of course it would have been better for me if I had divorced him."[27] And how much better for Violet Hunt.

In January of 1910, Ford moved into South Lodge, though the appearance of propriety was preserved by the fact that Hunt was living with her mother and charging Ford £3 a week for rent. Their establishment became the social center for the literary and bohemian crowd associated with *The English Review*. Pound was a frequent visitor, and Hunt's parrot was taught to squawk "Ezra, Ezra." Hunt gave her full support to the Vorticist movement, and Wyndham Lewis decorated with paint one of the drawing-room walls of South Lodge. When shortly before the war the young French artist, Henri Gaudier-Brzeska, sculpted a phallic white marble bust of Pound, the crowd invested it with magical power to ward off German bombs and placed it in the small front garden of South Lodge, where it remained for twenty years. Rebecca West, Brigit Patmore, and W. L. George joined Hunt's older friends, H. G. Wells, May Sinclair, and Ethel Colburn Mayne, as frequent guests, and the couple's annual garden parties were notable events. "Intellectual Hosts," Lewis once called Hunt and Ford, shrewdly observing that they belonged to "that valuable kind of human, who shuns solitude as the dread symbol of unsuccess, is happiest when his rooms are jammed with people (for preference of note)."[28] Hunt was certainly in her element. As for Ford, in 1910 Edward Garnett reported him as saying that he had found in his life at South Lodge more peace than he had known for twenty years.

Edwardian propriety, however, would not be flouted with impunity and such peace was necessarily illusory. For Hunt, there was the opprobrium of her family. Her mother, no longer a prolific novelist with a gift of conversation, but a difficult woman approaching senility, showed her disapproval of Ford and Pound by hiding their tennis shoes and rackets whenever Pound showed up for a game at South Lodge. Her Aunt Jane was convinced that Violet was squandering her mother's money in order to finance "a very giddy & godless life"[29] among the bohemians of London. And her married sisters (she calls them Goneril and Regan throughout her published memoirs) began under their aunt's influence a series of legal moves against Violet. When Margaret died in 1912 they contested her will, thereby withholding for four years money that Violet had been counting on. The hardest blow, however, was the estrangement of her favorite niece, Rosamond, whom she had begun to introduce into London society. One of Violet's friends commented that her maternal affection for her niece was almost painful to observe, but Violet's sister Silvia and her husband were conventional north-country people, who decided that South Lodge was no place for their daughter. Caught in the crossfire, Rosamond wrote explaining why she could no longer visit South Lodge, insisting that she loved her aunt but that she also loved her father, and hoping that Violet would not be cross.

Ford's problems also began to multiply. A plan for him to retain the editorship of *The English Review* under Mond's ownership fell through, and his separation from Elsie had estranged him from his children. "Fate was very hard on him," Hunt sympathized. "First the *Review*, then the children. After that January of 1911 I do not think he ever smiled much again."[30] Worse still, Ford and Hunt began tempting that Fate when on October 21 Ford was quoted by *The Daily Mirror* as saying that he had married Hunt in Germany, after divorcing his wife on the technical ground of desertion. Ford explained that he was able to take advantage of German law because he was heir to large Prussian estates and thus could still lay claim to German citizenship. Elsie could not have missed the headline: "Mr. Ford Madox Hueffer Married Abroad to Well-Known Lady Novelist." When she threatened to sue, the paper wisely ran a retraction. Not so wise was René Byles, business manager of *The Throne*, who called Violet "now Mrs. Hueffer" in announcing the publication of Margaret Hunt's *The Governess*, a novel which Ford helped Violet to complete after her mother's death in 1912. Ford and Hunt countered Elsie's threats of a suit by assuring Byles that they would stand by their claim in court if necessary. When Elsie did sue—and win— *The Throne* had to pay £1000 and was finished.

So was Violet Hunt. Despite their assurances to Byles, neither she nor Ford attended the trial, held on February 7, 1913. Ford had fled to Boulogne, and Hunt was left to cope with the consequences herself. So fully had she and Ford convinced themselves that they were in the right that it never crossed her mind that they and *The Throne* could lose, and the devastating result gave reality to fears she hardly dared to entertain. Nevertheless, Hunt was resilient and brazen. "The only thing for Ford & me to do is wipe the unjustifiable mud Elsie has thrown off our faces, make ourselves presentable & go on as if nothing had happened,"[31] she wrote Ford's mother. Ford, however, who hated publicity when he could not control it and present his own version of reality, simply went to pieces. Elsie commented to Olive Garnett that "Ford seems to be a wreck & V.H. is managing everything."[32] When Hunt reported the outcome of the case to Ford in Boulogne, and that Elsie's victory was being carried by every tabloid in London, he remained silent, refusing to listen to any details. He also began to drink heavily and to suffer symptoms of neurasthenia. Under a doctor's advice, Hunt led him from Montpellier, to Carcassonne, to Les Baux, to St. Rémy in the hopes of bringing him out of his depression.

Hunt's friends were not eager to see her return to England. One of them wrote to her suggesting that she stay abroad for three years: "I don't think you know *how strong* the feeling about you is, and it would be *impossible* for you to go about and be received without first asking what sort of reception you would get or whether you would get any at all."[33] Hunt responded characteristically that she assumed her friends would accept the legality of her "German marriage" and that they would treat all attacks on her reputation with the contempt they deserved. When she and Ford returned in the summer of 1913, her immediate tactic was to send out invitations to a party at South Lodge. Just as immediate was the response from her family: "According to the newspaper reports and statements, which I did hope you would have been able to refute *at once*, the mysterious divorce and subsequent marriage in Germany were mythical, and if so you can hardly expect continued support and partizanship from any of your relatives."[34]

Again and again, friends and relatives challenged Hunt to produce the documentary evidence of the divorce and marriage. Since no papers ever surfaced, Ford's biographers have agreed that the couple simply gambled that their bluff would not be called—and lost. Hunt is thus depicted as pitiful and tedious in her insistence on being called "Mrs. Hueffer" until the day she died. The evidence, however, suggests that there was indeed a marriage ceremony and that Violet was even more of a victim than has been recognized.

What is known and agreed upon is that Ford was told by a German lawyer that his father's own naturalization as an English citizen in 1872 would not make it impossible for Ford to resume German citizenship, although he would have to reside in Germany for about six months to show good faith.[35] Thereafter, the plan was to get a German divorce so that he and Violet could marry. The biographers' assumption is that, after several trying months in Giessen, he became impatient and in exasperation decided to simplify matters by returning home and just claiming they were married—after all, who would ever know the difference? The *Throne* case, the argument goes, thus easily exposed the couple's pretense and resulted in their public humiliation.[36] If this is indeed what happened, it is hard to understand how Ford and Hunt hoped to get away

19

with such a scheme. Would lovers who went to lengths to preserve appearances take such a risk, inviting a public court case (and the financial disgrace of their friend Byles) which they had no reason to believe they could win? Some further explanation seems called for.

To begin with, there is no question that both Ford and Hunt thought the plan feasible. After all, had not D. G. Rossetti written to Ford Madox Brown on the birth of his grandson, prophesying that the child would bring "glory to whichever of his two countries he may choose to adopt and that the other will have to mourn the eclipse of a leading luminary"?[37] Hunt herself began researching the life of Sir Herbert Herkomer, who married his sister-in-law after resuming German citizenship. More immediately, they could cite as precedent the case of Holman Hunt, and Violet had probably seen the Pre-Raphaelite painter's letters to her mother, touching upon his desire to marry his widow's sister, even though such a union was illegal in England.[38] Holman remarried in Holland, and when he returned to England with his new bride they overcame some censorious gossip and were fully accepted. With these precedents in mind, Hunt's good friends Dollie Radford and Ethel Mayne consulted a legal expert on her behalf.

Clearly something went wrong. Although Violet seems to have agreed willingly and knowingly to Ford's plan, she may have been duped by her co-conspirator into thinking that he had been naturalized as a German citizen. Or Violet's innocence of Ford's German affairs may have been a fiction the two of them agreed upon, playing their parts even in their letters to each other. At one point, Ford wrote Hunt from Germany to announce that his German lawyer thought it "all right now about the naturalization. . . . it is absolutely certain now. Isn't it jolly?"[39] When Hunt asked him to let her see the naturalization papers, Ford offered instead a series of unconvincing reasons for not being able to show them. Thus when Ford's mother wrote sharply to Hunt after the *Throne* scandal, she replied that "I only know what your son tells me of the German business."[40] By 1927, Ford was denying that he had ever become a German for any reason. And in 1930, Hunt wrote in the flyleaf of a book that "the plan was defeated by the inertia—or malice—of the male protagonist."[41]

Was there then no marriage ceremony as well as no naturalization? Hunt and Ford assured Byles that one had taken place in Hanover. However, Dame Rebecca West, who was a close friend and confidante of Hunt's at the time, asserted in a private interview that Hunt and Ford did indeed undergo a marriage ceremony, not in Germany, but in a hotel room in France.[42] Her claim is supported by an unpublished letter from Ford to Hunt in 1918, after he was confronted by his Commanding Officer with the old *Daily Mirror* interview in which he had claimed to be a German citizen and landowner. In it, Ford tells Hunt that he was asked why he had not revealed his German ties when he was applying for a commission. He answered that the question had not arisen, but that in any case he had shown allegiance to the King at the outbreak of the war and had been assured by the Home Office that his British nationality was not in question. Ford was also forced to deny that he possessed property in Prussia, as had been alleged in the *Mirror*. "Nothing else has passed," he assured Hunt. "I take it that these questions do not affect our marriage as that took place in France."[43]

If there was a ceremony in France, why did Hunt never announce it publicly, and why did she privately tell friends it took place in Germany? Perhaps she had good reason. When her friends consulted R. Ellis Roberts about the marriage plan, he warned them that it might open Ford to a charge of bigamy and that by English law Hunt would remain Ford's mistress, not his wife. Ethel Mayne and Dollie Radford asked Roberts to speak to Hunt, and he reluctantly agreed: "I told her the facts. . . . Nothing availed. Ford, she insisted, must be right; he was as anxious for marriage as she; it was his plan, after all he was very clever. The plan was wonderful."[44] However, what if, at some time between Ford and Hunt's assurance to Byles that they could fight Elsie in the courtroom and win, they were made to face the fact that to insist on their marriage would land them both into worse trouble than they had ever anticipated? Ford had already been called an adulterer—was he such an emotional wreck now because he feared being called something worse?

Let us go back to that letter from Hunt to Ford's mother to get Violet's explanation for not testifying in court: "I can't forget your eyes on that awful day when Elsie was swearing away all my reputation & I could do *nothing*. . . . I only know what your son tells me of the German business. I mean the divorce—that is his affair. Of course the marriage is mine & no one contested that, for of course Elsie wants to try and get Ford for bigamy. That is why I did not insist on going into court— for I might have been made to give date & place & witnesses. Now— nobody, not even you knows them."[45] And how could anyone ever find them out if, when Hunt did claim marriage, she placed it a country away from where it actually took place? A decade later, in the 1920s, in an intimate letter to Ethel Mayne, Hunt wrote: "if I could demonstrate my *bona fides* Ford would only be decried for having committed a bigamous

21

attempt for love of me! Not anything for a man to be ashamed of."[46] No papers of course have ever been found. A comment in the Foreword to *I Have This to Say*, significantly omitted from the English edition, suggests what she did with them. Apologizing for certain lacunae in her account of her legal problems, she writes: "I have been rudely taught since that it was not so—that I never did become a legal wife. And leave it at that, and the whole truth at the bottom of the well at Selsey where it may appropriately lie until the Peninsula is all at sea" (p. vi).

If there was a marriage, it was neither legal nor made in heaven, and Ford and Hunt were soon blaming each other for all their woes. Ford handled unpleasant reality either by evading it or by reshaping it imaginatively, and so he exasperated Hunt by his passivity in response to the turmoil. Hunt, on the other hand, always believed that she could confront her enemy by facing it down, and so to Ford's dismay she repeatedly made their affairs public by her constant need to justify herself. "He would bear quite meekly, like the 'exceedingly patient donkey' to which his father had compared him in boyhood, the weals of fate," Hunt wrote. "But I am different. I won't bear things unless I have to. I have to live always in the boiling middle of things, or, to mix metaphors, in a world of thin ice and broken eggs that will never make an omelette."[47] Moreover, by 1914, Hunt was accusing Ford of philandering, most particularly with her friend Brigit Patmore, with whom Ford was now infatuated. Hunt had shouldered all the costs of the lawyers' bills in the *Throne* case, and her money was used towards the support not only of Ford at South Lodge and in Germany but of his daughters and his estranged wife as well.[48] Hunt even paid for Ford's new teeth, claiming they might have been diamonds for what they cost her. By 1917, as her diary reveals, she was convinced that her only hold on him was financial. She may well have been right, for in that year Ford was once more in desperate financial straits, asking Edgar Jepson to arrange a loan for him of £50 to £100 through the Royal Literary Fund.

This was not the peace that Ford had hoped to get with Hunt. He hated scenes and wanted to hear none of her accusations. The vital, compelling woman of 1908 was now over fifty, obsessed with family quarrels, finances, and litigation, and a constant reminder of all his problems and failures. Moreover, he learned by 1915 that Hunt's previous experience of men, which in 1909 added to her mystery, had left her with tertiary syphilis. Although Hunt felt that Ford responded with outward tenderness and sympathy, according to Rebecca West she later believed he became somewhat repelled by her from the time he learned of her illness. As one of Ford's contemporaries remarked, what he really wanted now was "a nice, healthy girl who will admire him as he feels he deserves."[49] He needed to be pampered and comforted, not harangued by an aging, syphilitic woman with an acerbic tongue. And so, eventually, he bolted from Violet Hunt to Stella Bowen, who, after Ford had left her as well, could say that she considered her years with him "a privilege for which I am still trying to say thank you."[50] Feisty Violet Hunt was less grateful:

> I told him when he left me that he was no longer free like other men that if he found he couldn't bear to live with me, his only remedy before having let me into such an impasse was to cut his throat. I daresay you think this is North-country hardness. But if it had been me, I would have been 'the boy on the burning deck,' and stayed in South Lodge that he hates and saved my honour.[51]

Instead, in August of 1915 Ford secured a commission in the army and joined the Welch Regiment at Cardiff Castle. He thereby escaped not only the oppressive conditions at South Lodge but also the series of humiliations that had begun when Elsie abandoned her divorce proceedings. Ford was also at this point unhappy with the responses to *The Good Soldier*, published in March, and wondering whether he would ever write fiction again. He saw himself and his literary methods as no longer avant-garde, but rather middle-aged and disparaged by the young. By joining the army, he could slough off not only Hunt but the Hueffer-ian self with which she was associated. In uniform he became truly English, mentally as well as politically. He thus recreated himself as the good soldier in the King's uniform, Christopher Tietjens of his *Parade's End* tetralogy. When he returned from the war he would no longer be Ford Madox Hueffer. In explaining his change of name, Ford later said that Hueffer was "a name so suspect and unpronounceable that anyone bearing it might well expect without trial to be shot as a queer enemy spy."[52] Of course, it was not simply the unpronounceability of his German name that made Ford fear being shot at, but the suspicion that he retained German sympathies. And who was more responsible than Violet Hunt for this suspicion? After all, had it not been for her and her insistence on being married, he would never have hatched the plan which led him to tell reporters that he was a German citizen and landowner.

Ford had not helped matters when in 1914 he published a story in *The Bystander* called "The Scaremonger." The story was occasioned by an old friend of Hunt's, Edward Heron-Allen, who seven years earlier had shown a passionate interest in her. He became Hunt's landlord when he rented her his Knap cottage at Selsey. A bibliophile and a writer of impressively varied scientific and literary interests, Heron-Allen was also a superpatriot who joined the Intelligence Department of the War Office in 1918. He objected to Ford, probably as much because of Ford's relationship with Hunt as his Teutonic background. Ford in turn lost patience with Heron-Allen and his talk that Selsey was vulnerable to attack by the German fleet, and so satirized him as the scaremonger. Neither Hunt nor her friends were amused. "It seems to me artistically and—well, socially—a low thing," Brigit Patmore wrote Hunt. "I hated the little 'hits' against Richard [Aldington] and Hilda [Doolittle] that used to appear in the Outlook articles, but after all, they were only apparent to a very few, but the attack on Ned is flagrant, & all the more astounding as Ford always pretended to like Ned. Why did he do it?"[53]

The story, along with an article Ford wrote on "the gallant enemy" for *The Outlook*, only exacerbated the perception of the novelist as a German sympathizer. In January of 1915, the Chief Constable of West Sussex told Ford to leave the area of the Chichester division. The order was quickly withdrawn, but Ford denounced Hunt as the cause of these new problems through her indiscreet talk with friends and Selsey neighbors, and he berated her for not giving up those friends he held responsible. By June of 1919 he had rationalized his flight from Hunt as essentially her decision: "I gave Violet the choice between my leaving South Lodge or her giving up the acquaintanceship of certain people whom I regarded as my enemies. I found that she had been entertaining at Selsey the various gentlemen whose chief claim to patriotic activities, as you know, had been the denouncing of myself to the police as a German agent; and I also found that various other gentlemen were stating, on her authority, various other untruths to my disadvantage."[54] Even after Ford enlisted and served as an English officer his previously announced German loyalty hurt him professionally, and it certainly did Hunt no good in her attempts to hold on to Ford when a reviewer of their joint book, *Zeppelin Nights* (1916), accused Ford of being a foreigner and a coward and carried his prejudices over to his criticism: "There are flashes of Miss Hunt's genius dispersed throughout the volume, and one is sensible that she has made a heroic attempt to leaven the mass of Mr. Hueffer's dull offensiveness."[55]

Ford concealed from Hunt his decision to obtain a commission until it was a *fait accompli*. "V. takes it rather hard, poor dear, but I hope she will get used to the idea,"[56] he wrote his mother. On the evening of August 16, 1915, Hunt gathered some friends of Ford for a small send-off at South Lodge, a party which ended in a violent quarrel between Ford and Hunt after the other guests had left. From that point on, the affair was practically over. Hunt's 1917 diary depicts her subsequent sporadic meetings with Ford, still in uniform, at Selsey, London, Whitby, and Redcar. The diary suggests that, from her point of view particularly, the returning warrior was more insufferable than ever, and it confirms Goldring's speculation about Ford's attitude towards women after the war: "We can only guess that he felt that women owed him something and that, on various grounds, including his position as retired warrior, he was entitled to take what he wanted from them when he could get it."[57]

And so when Stella Bowen came along he took her. The 1917 diary shows for the first time that she entered Ford's circle as early as that year. By Armistice Day he was writing Bowen love letters, while meeting with accusations Hunt's appeals for him to return to South Lodge: "You drove me out of the house by insults—saying I only lived with you for the sake of money. I will not, I will not sleep in the house again."[58] When he left the army on January 1, 1919, he thus took separate lodgings at Campden Hill Gardens, although, persuaded in part by Bowen's urgings, he continued for the sake of appearances to receive his mail at South Lodge and to host jointly with Hunt the parties that resumed there in the twenties.

In her relentless jealousy and pursuit of Ford after he set up his household with Bowen, Hunt was exasperating. Goldring charitably suggests that she was temporarily out of her mind. Ford himself understood her psychology, as he treats it in the character of Sylvia in *The Last Post*:

> For it is to be remembered that one of the chief torments of the woman who has been abandoned by a man is the sheer thirst of curiosity for material details as to how that man subsequently lives. Sylvia Tietjens for a number of years had tormented her husband.... [She] had reason to believe that for many years, for better or for worse—and mostly for worse—she had been the dominating influence over Christopher Tietjens. Now, except for extraneous annoyances, she was aware that she could no longer influence him either for evil or for good.[59]

Nevertheless, Ford was greatly irritated by the "extraneous annoyances" that Hunt caused him, as when she brought May Sinclair with her to spy on his "love-in-a-cottage" life with Bowen, the two intruders peering over his gate while he fed his pigs. In August of 1920, Hunt even induced the wife of Ford's carpenter to send her news of her "husband," saying she was worried about his health. At first the woman wrote that she would be "only to [sic] pleased to let you know anything you wish to know about Capt Ford." Hunt told her that she, Violet, was Ford's true wife, while Stella, who was now calling herself Mrs. Ford, told the confused spy that Violet was really Ford's sister-in-law. By late October, the woman had apparently been found out, and, afraid of trouble, she returned Hunt's postage stamps, although she did write again in December to say that, as Hunt probably already knew, Mrs. Ford had (on November 29) given birth to a beautiful baby daughter, Esther Julia.[60]

The extent to which this incident irritated Ford is revealed by the animosity with which he treats Violet-Sylvia in *The Last Post*, when Sylvia similarly employs the carpenter's wife to spy on Tietjens: "Normally she would not—the members of her circle would not have—made confidantes of her ex-husband's domestics. But she had had to chance whether the details of Christopher's *menage* as revealed by the wife of his carpenter would prove to her friends sufficiently amusing to make them forget the social trespass she committed in consorting with her husband's dependants and she had to chance whether the carpenter's wife would not see that, by proclaiming her wrongs over the fact that her husband had left her, she was proclaiming her own unattractiveness."[61]

Moser has shown how Hunt appears in Ford's fiction during and after his relationship with her.[62] But it is as Sylvia in the Tietjens novels that Ford depicted her most obviously, most fully, and most viciously. "I do fancy, apart from her beauty, he has come to look on me as like that and it seems rather terrible but a matter of no importance really," Hunt wrote rather stoically to Ethel Mayne.[63] Perhaps Hunt was pleased that at least in his fiction Ford still acknowledged Sylvia-Violet as his wife, leaving a hint for posterity by placing their marriage ceremony in a Paris hotel bedroom.[64] (The autobiographical suggestion is made even stronger by the fact that Tietjens marries Sylvia on the rebound from Drake, a previous lover and, like Violet's Oswald Crawfurd, a married man who had taken advantage of her.) Nevertheless, insofar as Hunt saw in the novel Ford's version of their affair, it is hard to believe she took as calmly as her comment to Mayne suggests "the terrifying story of a good man tortured, pursued, driven into revolt, and ruined as far as the world is concerned by the clever devices of a jealous and lying wife."[65] There for all the world to see was Violet as Sylvia, "too old for Christopher," telling Tietjens, when he takes up with Valentine-Stella: "I never did have much opinion of your taste. . . . Put her back. She's too young for you."[66] There she is making scenes, to the distaste of the superior Tietjens, who would "rather be dead than an open book."[67] And there she is, hounding her man and distracting him from the important soldiering he has chosen instead of her. Goldring could have been judging the Sylvia of *No More Parades* when he said of Violet: "Why *did* she have to go on trying to wring his heart-strings, even after he had joined his regiment and began his training for the ghastly ordeal ahead of him? Alas, she could never escape from herself or look beyond the circumference of her own griefs. No cataclysm was great enough to enable her to forget, even for a moment, her own sorrows out of sympathy for the suffering of others."[68]

In the Tietjens novels, Ford thus indirectly accuses Hunt of sole responsibility for the failure of their relationship. Whereas Tietjens is "a fellow who never told a lie or did a dishonourable thing in his life," all Sylvia's acts are "perpetrated under the impulsion of sex-viciousness." Her indiscriminate tongue set in motion the lies that resulted in Mark's estrangement from his brother. "If you wanted something killed you'd go to Sylvia Tietjens in the sure faith that she would kill it: emotion, hope, ideal; kill it quick and sure. If you wanted something kept alive you'd go to Valentine." In his disappointment with Violet, Ford calls Sylvia a thoroughbred who has somehow turned into a vicious mare. Sylvia's aggressive possessiveness thus drives Tietjens into the army, as he joins thinking that "the best thing for him was to go and get wiped out as soon as possible." He thinks of returning to Sylvia as a return to Hell, as if God had devised for him "a cavernous eternity of weary helplessness."[69]

If Hunt was hurt by this portrait of Ford's attitude toward her, she was probably furious over the way he inverted some of the terms of their relationship in order to suit his imaginative needs. As opposed to his promiscuous bitch of a wife, Tietjens stands for chastity and monogamy: "The lady, Mrs. Tietjens, was certainly without mitigation a whore, he himself equally certainly and without qualification had been physically faithful to the lady and their marriage tie."[70] So Tietjens heroically refrains from taking Valentine to bed before he leaves for the service because "We're the sort that . . . *do not*!"[71] At the same time, he magnanimously takes Sylvia back when she decides to end her adulterous fling with Perowne. Yet in life it was always Hunt who took Ford back after his flings, whether with Brigit Patmore or the Miss Ross they quarrel about in her 1917 diary, and it was not until the end of their affair that Hunt records her "first infidelity" to Ford. She might well have felt that if some do, Ford always did, and if some do not, it was she who usually showed emotional and sexual commitment.

It is possible that Ford was working out some other feelings toward Hunt in suggesting Sylvia's promiscuity so strongly. Perhaps she was a

27

"whore" like Sylvia not because she was unfaithful to him, but because of her past, particularly after Ford discovered from her doctor that she had contracted syphilis from a previous affair. Mizener suggests that this knowledge may have gone into Ford's portrait of Florence in *The Good Soldier*. Even more likely, it relates to Sylvia and Tietjens's obsession with the idea that when he married her she may have been pregnant with the child of her previous lover. Sylvia's affair with Perowne would thus objectify not only her promiscuity but also the earlier affairs of Hunt by which Ford was now repelled. Certainly Hunt's illness must have been in Ford's mind when in *The Last Post* he has Sylvia invent the tale that Mark's paralysis is a result of his youthful sexual aberrations. In her self-absorption, however, Sylvia does not realize the extent of Mark's illness: "Of course the results of venereal disease are not pleasant to contemplate and no doubt Sylvia having invented the disease for him had not liked to contemplate the resultant symptoms."[72]

Ford also transforms in his fiction the financial relationship between him and Hunt. Whereas Sylvia is financially dependent on Tietjens, who supports both her and her mother, in life Ford and his estranged family receive money from Hunt. Ford lived off of Hunt and her aged mother at South Lodge, but in the Tietjens novels South Lodge is transformed into Groby, Tietjens's family estate, which he grandly turns over to Sylvia: "As far as he was concerned Groby was entirely at her disposal with all that it contained. And of course a sufficient income for the upkeep."[73] The Ford who was always in debt, borrowing from friends and accusing publishers of not doing enough to sell his books, becomes in these novels the privileged Christopher Tietjens, who lends money to Macmaster without expecting repayment, who refuses his father's legacy, who chooses on principle the poverty that Ford could not avoid.

Of course Ford never claimed to be treating life. He depicted and transformed his relations with Hunt in these novels not because he shared her need to defend her conduct against criticism by the outside world, but because he was an artist who needed to reconstruct reality in ways that allowed him to accept it and himself. And perhaps what he needed most was what Violet would not give him but Sylvia finally gave Tietjens —a kind of forgiveness and a willingness to let him get on with his new life—since Sylvia decides she will not stand in the way of a baby and grants Tietjens a divorce so he can marry the pregnant Valentine. Violet, however, was no more ready to grant Ford a "divorce" than was Elsie, and she held to the end her conviction that he was bound until the last post was sounded to honor his promises and commitment to her.

Even though Ford had a romantic need to reimagine his life in his fiction, there is no reason for the literary historian to see him as he saw himself, as Martin Seymour-Smith clearly does: "No man was more persecuted by women—Ford suffered unreasonably from his wife, but more from the woman he left her for, Violet Hunt—and he was lucky to find some happiness with Stella Bowen and then even more, in the last nine years of his life, with Janice Biala."[74] Hunt's 1917 diary shows that, although she willfully inflicts pain on Ford, she too "suffered unreasonably" at his hands. One wonders at the double standard which still allows the contemporary critic to conflate in a sentence the four women whom the novelist loved and left, and yet represent him as wholly the victim. Ford boasted of his sympathies with the suffragists and chose for himself artistic and intelligent women, but he always assumed that their role was to serve genius. As Goldring writes approvingly, "If man's primary function is the creation of life and woman's its transmission it seemed not unnatural to him that the creative artist should have a woman by his side to take care of the offspring of his brain and look after the minor details of his daily life—run his home, type for him, entertain his friends, ward off duns and tell him when to buy a new hat." From that point of view, Ford's problem was simply that he did not marry the right kind of woman to begin with: "Within the confines of conventional matrimony, no one nowadays [1943]—not even his wife, unless she was a fool— would have grudged him a concubine or two, when inspiration flagged."[75]

We see the double standard operating for Ford in *Some Do Not . . .*, when Tietjens refuses to let Sylvia's adulterous affair be known even though it leads to slanderous talk about himself: "If there were, in clubs and places where men talk, unpleasant rumours as to himself he preferred it to be thought that he was the rip, not his wife the strumpet. That was normal, male vanity; the preference of the English gentleman! . . . It was better for a boy to have a rip of a father than a whore for mother!"[76] Of course it is better, since at worst the man is a "rip" while the woman is a "whore." Perhaps no incident in Ford's biography better illustrated his own assumption of a double standard than when he first left Elsie to seek his fortune in South Kensington. He had already been unfaithful to her with her sister and was now embarking on his affair with Hunt, when Elsie wrote that Ford's friend Marwood was making advances. Ford's indignation was instantaneous: "I must confess that your letter—as far as it affects Marwood—rather astonishes me. If it be true that he has attacked yr virtue and my honour (which is what it amounts to) I cannot for the sake of business have any friendly relations with him."[77] It is always the man's honor and the maid's virtue that are at stake—never the reverse. Even contemporary biographers seem to accept the terms. Without questioning Ford's reaction to Marwood's advances, Mizener writes of Elsie, "She persisted during this period in attacking Ford, in a gloomy and violent way, about the life he was leading in London and in asserting her ill-directed but justified jealousy of the women he was seeing."[78] Despite the suggestion of "justified," the terms "attacking," "gloomy," "violent," "persisted," "asserting," "ill-directed," and "jealousy" reveal the biographer's bias. When Thomas Moser pointed out to Rebecca West that Ford fell in love every five years and could not stay attached more than ten, she replied tartly: "This seems to me characteristic of many of your sex and cannot, I think, be counted as an idiosyncrasy of Ford."[79]

III. The Larger Context and the Rest of the Story

When Moser charts the coincidence of these phases with the decades and half-decades of Ford's life, it becomes clear that Hunt never stood a chance. Incapable of what she admired in his friend Conrad, the "sense of responsibility in emotional affairs,"[80] Ford simply assumed the transience of love, noting that every person in the modern world has his "passionate experiences" during which there will be moments when he or she "will be alive to the member of the opposite sex who for the time being attracts him."[81] So when the "time being" of his early life was over, he left Elsie to begin a new phase as editor and man about town in literary London with Hunt. And when it was time to become the British soldier and afterwards the small producer, Hunt's "time being" was over and Bowen's began—until she too gave way to Janice Biala when Ford entered his last phase as the blessed headmaster of a coterie of disciples in Paris and New York. (There were literary benefits of all these changes as well, since as Moser points out each time Ford embarked on a major new novel about modern life, he drew courage from a new woman.) From the point of view of Ford's women, then, he was more victimizer than victim, what Bowen called a "great user-up of other people's nervous energy."[82] In retrospect Hunt defined accurately the kind of love

Ford had to offer: "Love without breadth, depth, or thickness, without dimension. Subjective, purely. For the object—set up like an ikon to be worshipped, perfunctorily, with genuflections and lip-service, a queen in the game of knights and castles—any sort of fetish, glittering, shining, compelling, will do."[83]

If the story of Hunt's relationship with Ford acquires a sense of inevitability as we understand its internal tensions and his emotional needs, it takes on even more of one when we stand back and view it as the completion of a pattern established much earlier in Hunt's life. In her relations with two other married men, as well as with a number of more eligible suitors, Hunt established the patterns of behavior that destroyed her. She sought, quite purposefully, flirtations and intrigues with men who were either unavailable or unsuitable, and usually both. The more dangerous the men, the more hotly she pursued them. Eventually, her affairs drew disapproval from her family and gossip from friends as they became public knowledge, invariably through her own deliberate indiscretion. And as they died down, she desperately tried to fan them up again by the wholly ineffective tactic of berating her lovers and talking too much to everyone, thereby exacerbating the unpleasantness for herself, her lovers, her friends, and her family. While she pursued her own destruction, she toyed with the affections of more appropriate suitors, briefly admiring their solidity and the respectability they could offer, before dismissing them as dull.

Her first major affair, aside from some crushes on older men and flirtations with younger ones, was with the painter George Boughton, who lived on Campden Hill Road in West House, near the Hunts' Tor Villa. In 1882 Hunt began sitting for Boughton, when she was only twenty and Boughton forty-nine, old enough to be her father and with a daughter her own age. Although at this stage of their acquaintance she was properly chaperoned whenever she sat for him, by the following year she was posing regularly in his studio, walking with him whenever possible, fleeing when others intruded, and provoking his daughter Flossie's suspicion. Older and wiser than the impetuous Violet, Boughton was reluctant to have his reputation tarnished by his neighbor's reckless daughter, whom he lectured "on necessary Mrs Grundyisms."[84]

Their affair began in 1884 and continued for several years, but by 1887 Mrs. Boughton's patience wore thin and she sharply claimed her straying husband. At that point, he broke off the relationship with Violet, and Mrs. Hunt packed her tearful daughter off to Robin Hood's Bay in Yorkshire, where she consoled herself by flirting with a young boy of only sixteen or seventeen, Euty Strickland. Upon her return that fall, she enacted another dramatic parting scene with Boughton: "Met George, and oh, how bitter! I reviled him for being a slave to his wife, and for treating me so badly, and *left* him." Dramatics aside, at this point we might wonder who left whom.[85]

Hunt's flirtation with Euty Strickland seemed to embarrass his family, who were not pleased to have their son visited at Eton by a twenty-five-year-old woman, and they put a stop to any correspondence between them. By May Hunt had effected a temporary reconciliation with Boughton, but not to the exclusion of other suitors, who were at this point plentiful. None of these flirtations amounted to anything except too much gossip, and Hunt ended the year under a cloud of disapproval by her family, who were shocked at her fickleness: "Aunt A. says I have not the adumbration of a moral principle!"[86] Certainly, this was not the last time Violet was to hear that accusation. "Sometimes I do feel as if I had devastated and laid waste the family visiting list," the young Hunt mused.

When two more appropriate suitors, D. S. MacColl and Dr. Cholmely, competed for her attentions, both of them evidently encouraged by dinner invitations from her parents, Hunt was only briefly intrigued by them. MacColl she acknowledged to be good looking and clever, but he was too cool and self-contained for her; she called him "the stately MacColl." And Cholmely, whose main attraction seemed to be his library, she dismissed as the "faithful available." Even after her younger sisters married, Violet could not bring herself to face the future: "Had a long talk with S[ilvia] about my sad little *avenir*. Dear me, to be Aunt Violet, and make frocks for the children, only it is a pity that I have the *allures de femme mariée* so they say, and I am used to affection, do not know how I shall accommodate myself without it as is inevitable—youth and beauty departed—However, I can truly say I have had a good time." Thus by cultivating the thrill of the moment and rejecting men like Cholmely, her "legitimate prey," Hunt continued to live dangerously, get herself talked about, and alienate the society whose approval she needed. Even in her youth she enacted the same pattern of defiance she did with Ford.[87]

With the arrival on the scene of her next lover, Oswald Crawfurd, Hunt began to recognize the pattern in her life: "G[eorge] initiated me into the secret of what I *could* feel and has now left me—*inassouvie*." If respectable men like Cholmely and MacColl could not satisfy Hunt's craving for excitement, Oswald Crawfurd was a more promising candidate. An Oxford-educated dabbler in literature and publishing, Crawfurd had served as British consul to Oporto from 1869-1892 but spent half of each year living in London, where he was an editor of *The Novel Magazine* and a director of the journal *Black & White*, as well as an active participant in London society. Like Boughton, he too was a married man, but his wife was conveniently ill, leaving him free to pursue his romantic interests. By the time he became attracted to Hunt, she was well aware of her own predilection for married men and unsuitable relationships. Long before she and Crawfurd actually became lovers, she wrote in her diary: "There would be something very ridiculous in my being engaged for a second time in an intrigue with a married man."[88]

Crawfurd, however, was less willing than Boughton to be drawn into an affair on Violet's terms. She found him puzzling and disturbing: in his letters to her he wrote "odd things" and expressed "wild notions of free love." Although she and Crawfurd were not yet lovers in 1890, she knew what their future held. Upon meeting Boughton again and pressing hands with him, she stifled the impulse to blurt out, "I've got another. What shall I do with him?"[89] But if Hunt paused to wonder what to do with her next conquest, it was not for long, and once she decided to reject Cholmely and MacColl, there was no turning back. The affair with Crawfurd went on openly, to her family's dismay, from 1892 to 1898, but even though Crawfurd's wife could not yank him back as Boughton's could, neither could Hunt secure him as she wanted to. When his wife finally died in 1899 he married again, not Violet, but one of her friends, Lita Brown.

Crawfurd's letters to Hunt at the end of their affair convey his exasperation with her talkativeness and his conviction—one that Ford was also later to express—that her tongue was damaging him. In a letter admitting his financial straits and his need to write for money, he admonished her: "You need not mention all this unless indeed your desire to do harm is greater than your desire not to—when you have your opportunity! Forgive the innuendo, but you know you *do* talk." Like Boughton before and Ford afterwards, Crawfurd had no confidence in Hunt's self-control and discretion: "I love you dear, but am a little afraid of you." And later his tone, again anticipating Ford's, turned positively hostile and accusatory: "You cannot be with me without scolding and reproaching me and finding fault with me—you had not been five minutes in my company before you began. You say rude and wounding things that in my present state of health are absolutely unendurable to me."[90]

Hunt permitted none of her affairs to end cleanly. This time her parents packed her off to Paris to recover, and she stayed for several years before returning to England. And even then she continued to talk. Her novel *Soonor or Later* (1904) recounts the sordid emotional details of her affair with Crawfurd in a thinly disguised *roman à clef*, accusatory of the manipulative "Robert Assheton," but equally hard on her fictional counterpart, the "ingenious ingenue" who craves excitement but when the affair wanes presents herself in the room "like an unpaid bill." Thus in the Crawfurd affair as well as in the later Ford affair, Hunt's desperation knew no discretion.

By 1905 Hunt discovered that the spots on her face were symptoms of tertiary syphilis, acquired from Crawfurd. Time had caught up with her, and by now she had repeated once too often the cycle of daring flirtation, affair with a man unsuitable by age and marital status, prolonged recrimination, and rejection of respectability. By the time she joined Ford and the *English Review* circle in 1908, she was no longer young and respectability no longer hers to reject. When Crawfurd died in 1909, she sentimentally pasted his obituary in her diary and made herself ready for her next assault. Once again there was an unlikely difference in age, although this time the man was younger than herself and she was the more experienced party. But the pattern proved strong: again she could neither bring her affair to the culmination she desired nor allow it to end without bitterness and embarrassment.

After Ford left Hunt, she did not resume her cycle of grand passions and bitter partings. For one thing, she was no longer young and resilient; for another, she did not admit defeat openly, as her continued use of Ford's name attests. Nevertheless, she knew, at some level, that the game was up for her, that she had failed to obtain the one thing she desperately wanted—someone to share the remainder of her life with her at South Lodge. We see this recognition of defeat emerging in the pages of her 1917 diary, and as the years went on, her awareness increased. Thus she conceded in *The Flurried Years*, "I seemed to have drawn a blank . . . in happiness. No Rewards and Fairies for me, no hope of the romantic millenium of which I had dreamed, of sentimental and satisfactory adjustments of joy or, at least, amenity all round, that many indications had led me to hope."[91] But even in defeat Hunt was a determined preserver of appearances. Goldring recalls seeing her at a cocktail party in the summer of 1924: "She was then over sixty, but anyone who saw her for the first time and noted how the young men crowded round her and laughed at her sallies would have supposed her to be at least twenty years younger. She was the centre of attraction, a regular 'honey pot,' sparkling, flirtatious and lavishly endowed with sex appeal. 'The brave old dear!' murmured a man who had known her as long as I had, as we watched her flash her still lovely eyes at the youth who was handing her a cocktail. 'She *does* keep her end up!'"[92]

The "brave old dear" who kept up social appearances also kept up her literary career, which always directly reflected her emotional and amorous interests. After the Ford affair ended, Hunt continued work on the second of her autobiographical novels, *Their Hearts*, dealing with her relationships with her sisters as they passed from adolescence to maturity, and she also wrote a novel, *The Last Ditch* (1921), exploring the impact of the war. She continued to write stories of the supernatural type that had first won her praise ("Tales of the Uneasy," she called them) and published a second volume of these tales in 1925. In several of these stories, "Love's Last Leave" and "The Corsican Sisters" in particular, she dealt with the two subjects that obsessed her: the impact of war on the women left behind and the propensity of men, especially artists, to exploit women. In addition to fiction, Hunt turned for the first time to the memoir, and in 1926 published *The Flurried Years*, a work which may be seen as her counter to Ford's imaginative recreation of their relationship in the *Parade's End* novels. Where he transformed life into fiction, she insisted on telling her own story in her own way—cryptically, allusively, with names disguised according to her own private code. Throughout her memoir, she refers to Ford by his Germanic name, Joseph Leopold—a reminder of the connection he had by then so entirely rejected. Hunt's final literary project was a biography of Elizabeth Sidall, *The Wife of Rossetti* (1932), in which she returns to her own (and Ford's) Pre-Raphaelite roots to accuse Rossetti of exploiting his wife and driving her to her death.

But Hunt never acquired as much literary recognition as she hoped for in her final years. In her lonely last decade fewer and fewer people called on her at South Lodge, and her mind deteriorated from both old age and the effects of disease. Those who knew her at that time recall her as garrulous, forgetful, and embarrassing, while she gradually lost her hold on reality. To make matters even more uncomfortable, she was often aware of her own decline. In 1935 she wrote pathetically to Goldring: "Do come & see me *soon* again. I *am* so lonely—so *desorientée* in life. It's not there *for me* any more!"[93] By the time London was enduring the blitz of World War II, she was completely confused, unable to distinguish this war from the first, the present nightmare from the past. In her muddle, she regressed to her childhood, confusing the sound of the bombs with thunder in the Welsh mountains that she used to visit with her father and needing constant reassurance that she was safe in her own home. Violet Hunt died in 1942, having experienced two wars, outliving her mental faculties as well as her passion for Ford. Although damaged by the air raids of World War II, South Lodge still stands. The only plaque on it announces that it was once the residence of Ford Madox Ford.

Unlike Ford, who wanted to forget the past once he successfully re-imagined it, Hunt's ambition was to remember and to be remembered. To that end, she spent her final years going over her papers and diaries, trying to continue her literary research, maintain her friendships, and dispose of her belongings to people she thought would value them. On the whole, she was unsuccessful. She died in poverty and obscurity, and her one memorial, a novel by Norah Hoult titled *There Were No Windows* (1946), tells her story under the name of Clair Temple, once a brilliant and witty novelist, who is shown in decline from senility to death.[94] As one who insisted on telling her own story, Hunt would have been glad her 1917 diary survived her.

I am so awkward with him that no position
is tenable. I believe we ought to part. I
shall perhaps be strong enough to will him
to that effect when I am away.
Thursday It's very dull.
Friday 31 A row, because I say I want
to go home on Sat! He "resents it —as an
insult to him." He is mad. I mean to
not to care. I have to get it into my head
that he is oblique .... I agreed late at
night to stay till Monday
Saturday Spent a rainy morning
in undoing all my arrangements
for home. A row with F. that night
Sunday I ought not to have stayed
We entertained largely all day. The
Haggards (Major, Second in Command) to
Dinner. Billiards. Then F. wanted
to sleep with one in the literal sense
"cushy & agreeable" — I tried to arouse

Photocopy of a page from Violet Hunt's 1917 diary. Courtesy of the Pennsylvania State University Libraries.

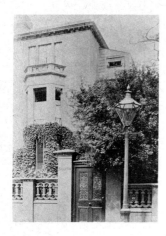

South Lodge.
Hunt's house in South
Kensington,
where she lived
with Ford
from 1910 to 1915.

Violet Hunt as a young girl.

Ford (right) at Cap Martin, from which he returned to Violet in 1917.

Hunt's cottage at Selsey.

Ford (seated center), Hunt (second from left), Brigit Patmore (left), and friends at the Selsey Hotel.

Ford and Rebecca West at Selsey.

Hunt, West, and Ford, with West's baby, Anthony.

Brigit Patmore and H. G. Wells.

Ford and Hunt relaxing at Selsey.

Ford and Hunt at the Selsey Hotel.

Edward Heron-Allen.

Canon William Greenwell.

Ford in 1909-10.

Violet Hunt in 1904.

Brigit Patmore.

Stella Bowen.

DESCRIPTION OF THE DIARY
AND EDITORIAL PROCEDURE

Violet Hunt's 1917 diary occupies 93 pages, recto and verso, in a 6¾"
x 8" notebook, hard bound, with blue marbled endpapers. The first entry
in it is for February 24, 1917, and the last for January 24, 1918. This
diary had become separated from the bulk of the Hunt papers, which
Arthur Mizener brought to Cornell; therefore, it was unavailable to him
when he completed his definitive biography of Ford, published in 1971.
The diary is now the property of the Pattee Library, of The Pennsylvania
State University Libraries. It is written in black ink, with several small
insertions added in either pencil or darker ink. We present here the
complete text of the diary. The only change we made was to standardize
the dating for the convenience of the reader, since Hunt herself does not
always supply both day and date. We have retained Hunt's punctuation,
even when it is eccentric. We have, however, inserted the missing quotation mark when she supplied only one of a pair. All ellipses and ditto
marks are hers. When Hunt's additions represent later commentary on
events, we have incorporated such interpretive afterthoughts in brackets,
prefaced by her initials.

In annotating the diary, we attempted to identify all public figures—
authors, artists, politicians, academic and military associates—indicating
when relevant their particular accomplishments around 1917 and their
relationship to Ford and Hunt. We sometimes include a statement about
these figures' private lives where they serve as reflectors upon the Ford-
Hunt relationship.

NOTES

[1] Letters from Henry James to Violet Hunt, August 28, 1907, and January 6, 1906, in the University of Virginia Library.

[2] Douglas Goldring, *Life Interests* (London: Macdonald & Co., 1948), p. 172.

[3] *Letters of Ford Madox Ford*, ed. Richard M. Ludwig (Princeton: Princeton University Press, 1965), p. 66.

[4] See diary annotation for October 2, 1917.

[5] Violet Hunt, *I Have This To Say* (New York: Boni and Liveright, 1926), p. 73.

[6] Violet Hunt, *The Flurried Years* (London: Hurst & Blackett, 1926), p. 80. This is the English edition of *I Have This To Say*, but there are a number of differences between the two books, and passages which appear in one do not always appear in the other.

[7] Allen Tate, "FMF," *New York Review of Books*, I, 2 (Spring/Summer 1963), rpt. in Sondra Stang, *The Presence of Ford Madox Ford* (Philadelphia: University of Pennsylvania Press, 1981), p. 13.

[8] Quotations in this paragraph are from *Some Do Not . . .*, pp. 32, 121; *No More Parades*, p. 396; *The Last Post*, p. 731; *No More Parades*, pp. 381, 429 (New York: Random House, 1979).

[9] See Robert Secor, *John Ruskin and Alfred Hunt: New Letters and the Record of a Friendship*, No. 25, ELS (British Columbia: University of Victoria, 1982).

[10] "The carefully shaded portrait heads by Miss Violet Hunt show unmistakably her affiliation to the Pre-Raphaelite brotherhood" (*The Observer*, December 2, 1931).

[11] Ford Madox Ford, *It Was the Nightingale* (Philadelphia: J. B. Lippincott Co., 1933), p. 49.

[12] *The Flurried Years*, p. 26.

[13] Arthur Mizener, *The Saddest Story: A Biography of Ford Madox Ford* (New York: The World Publishing Co., 1971), p. 177.

[14] Margaret Drabble, *Arnold Bennett* (New York: Knopf, 1974), p. 110.

[15] Drabble, p. 110, and *The Flurried Years*, p. 45.

[16] *Life Interests*, p. 172.

[17] Lawrence to Garnett, February 10, 1912, in *The Collected Letters of D. H. Lawrence*, ed. Moore (New York: The Viking Press, 1961), I, pp. 98-99.

[18] This undated letter is at Cornell. For a discussion of Hunt's fiction, see Marie Secor, "Violet Hunt, Novelist," *English Literature in Transition*, 19 (1976), 25-34; also Marie and Robert Secor, "Violet Hunt's Tales of the Uneasy," *Women and Literature*, 6 (Spring 1978), 16-27.

[19] Wells to Hunt, undated; Galsworthy to Hunt, March 12, 1908; Sinclair to Hunt, March 24, 1908. All at the Cornell University Library. There are other letters at Cornell congratulating Hunt on the achievement of her novel from R. B. Cunninghame Graham, André Raffalovich, W. J. Locke, Reginald Turner, and Albert Fleming.

[20] Joyce also commented that Ford's six wives were only one shy of Earwicker's in *Finnegans Wake*; Richard Ellmann, *James Joyce* (New York: Oxford University Press, 1965), p. 649.

[21] Stella Bowen, *Drawn from Life* (London: Collins, 1941), p. 62.

[22] Robert Secor, "Aesthetes and Pre-Raphaelites: Oscar Wilde and the Sweetest Violet in England," *Texas Studies in Literature and Language*, 21, No. 3 (1979), 403.

[23] Ford to Hunt, August 5, 1909; June 12, 1909; August (n.d.), 1909. Hunt to Ford, August 3 and 4, 1909. Cornell University Library

[24] David Garnett, *The Golden Echo* (London: Chatto & Windus, 1953), p. 183.

[25] Hunt reproduces the James letter in *The Flurried Years*, p. 88, but with some changes and inaccuracies. The original is at the University of Virginia Library. Her reply is here published for the first time, from a copy of it among her papers at Cornell.

[26] *I Have This To Say*, pp. 84-85.

[27] Mizener, p. 191.

[28] Mizener, p. 228.

[29] *The Flurried Years*, p. 103.

[30] *The Flurried Years*, p. 157.

[31] Mizener, p. 232.

[32] Olive Garnett's diary entry for June 18, 1912. In Thomas Moser, *The Life in the Fiction of Ford Madox Ford* (Princeton: Princeton University Press, 1980), p. 100.

[33] Douglas Goldring, *South Lodge* (London: Constable & Co., 1943), p. 108.

[34] *South Lodge*, p. 112.

[35] In her unpublished papers at Cornell, Hunt notes that Ford divorced Elsie "in Germany for Desertion Defamation, as a German who has got nationality or never forfeited it (for he was sixteen when his father became a

B[ritish] citizen) and became a German subject [by his brief residence in Germany] can."

36 *South Lodge*, p. 97, and Mizener, p. 230.

37 The unpublished letter from Rossetti to Brown, dated December 17, 1873, is in the Berg Collection at the New York Public Library.

38 These letters are now among the Hunt papers at Cornell.

39 *The Flurried Years*, p. 182.

40 Mizener, p. 232.

41 *South Lodge*, p. 130.

42 Dame Rebecca West in an interview with Marie Secor, in London, January 1977.

43 Ford to Hunt, May 12, 1918. Cornell University Library.

44 Mizener, p. 204.

45 Mizener, p. 232.

46 Violet Hunt to Ethel Colburn Mayne, ca. 1925. Private collection of Edward Naumberg, Jr.

47 *The Flurried Years*, p. 123.

48 In her unpublished papers at Cornell, Hunt writes: "Byles began to send Elsie my cheque for alimony regularly (£3 a week) on March 23rd 1911 —she would not receive it from me."

49 *South Lodge*, p. 115.

50 Bowen, p. 165.

51 Hunt to Mayne, ca. 1925, Naumberg.

52 *It Was The Nightingale*, p. 136.

53 Patmore to Hunt, December 30, 1914. Cornell University Library.

54 Ford to F. G. Masterman, June 1919, in Douglas Goldring, *The Last Pre-Raphaelite* (London: Macdonald & Co., 1948), p. 202.

55 J. K. Prothero in *New Witness*, vii, January 6, 1916, 293.

56 Mizener, p. 280.

57 *The Last Pre-Raphaelite*, p. 202.

58 Mizener, p. 302.

59 *The Last Post*, pp. 788-89.

60 These letters from R. Hunt are in the Cornell University Library.

61 *The Last Post*, p. 789.

62 Moser sees aspects of Ford's relation to Hunt in *A Call* (1910), *The Portrait* (1910), *Ladies Whose Bright Eyes* (1911), *The Good Soldier* (1915), *The Young Lovall* (1913), and *The Marsden Case* (1923).

[63] Hunt to Mayne, ca. 1925, Naumberg. In the American edition of her published memoirs, however, Hunt disingenuously suggests that she has more in common with the sympathetically drawn heroine of the tetralogy, Valentine Wannop, particularly insofar as she was similarly a suffragist. (*I Have This To Say*, p. 203.)

[64] *Some Do Not . . .*, p. 149.

[65] Graham Greene, Introduction to Volume III of *The Bodley Head Ford Madox Ford* (London: 1963), p. 5. Greene calls Sylvia "surely the most possessed evil character in the modern novel" (p. 6).

[66] *The Last Post*, p. 740, and *No More Parades*, p. 342.

[67] *No More Parades*, p. 342.

[68] *South Lodge*, p. 118.

[69] *Some Do Not . . .*, p. 226; *The Last Post*, p. 730; *Some Do Not . . .*, pp. 128, 224, and 120.

[70] *No More Parades*, p. 343.

[71] *Some Do Not . . .*, p. 224.

[72] *The Last Post*, p. 728.

[73] *No More Parades*, p. 430.

[74] Martin Seymour-Smith, *Guide to Modern World Literature* (New York: Funk & Wagnalls, 1973), p. 206.

[75] *South Lodge*, p. 231.

[76] *Some Do Not . . .*, pp. 76-77.

[77] Mizener, p. 182.

[78] Mizener, p. 181.

[79] Moser, p. 119.

[80] *The Flurried Years*, p. 13.

[81] *Men and Women* (Paris: Three Mountains Press, 1923), p. 36.

[82] Bowen, p. 83.

[83] *The Flurried Years*, p. 219.

[84] From Hunt's unpublished diaries at the Cornell University Library: April 24, 26, and May 2, 1882; and May 7, 1884.

[85] From diary entries of July 6 and October 21, 1887.

[86] From diary entries of February 18 and June 12, 1889.

[87] From diary entries of November 3 and October 17, 1889, and August (n.d.) 1890. Douglas Sutherland MacColl (1859-1948) was a well-known Scottish painter, art historian, critic, and curator of both the Tate Gallery and the Wallace Collection.

[88] From diary entries of September 22, August 11, September 8, and August 5, 1890.

[89] From diary entries of August 31, October 4, and December 30, 1890.

[90] Oswald Crawfurd to Violet Hunt, October 23, 1898; November 3, 1898; n.d., ca. 1898. Cornell University Library.

[91] *The Flurried Years*, p. 96.

[92] *South Lodge*, p. 135.

[93] *South Lodge*, p. 196. Another young acquaintance of Hunt's recalls, "I used to see her from time to time at parties, looking beautiful but haggard. On the very last occasion—it was somewhere on Campden Hill—I said 'I must go now or I shall be late for the children's bedtime' (they were 8 and 6) and she replied very sadly 'Oh how lucky you are to have children to go back to—all I shall return to is a cross cook and a boiled egg.'" Renée Haynes to Robert Secor, May 3, 1977.

[94] Norah Hoult's remarkable book gives a painful and accurate portrait of Hunt in her decline. Hoult herself says she meant to stay true to the original in her recreation of Violet as Clair, and that "it is safe to draw on my novel" for biographical details. Hoult remembers Hunt as "a charming warm-hearted person, though foolish also in a very feminine way." She recalls "Frank Swinnerton, my other literary friend, saying he was sorry I hadn't been able to give much impression of Violet's sweetness and gaiety." Norah Hoult to Robert Secor, July 18, 1978.

Violet Hunt's Diary

February 24, 1917, to January 24, 1918

Sat., Feb. 24.   While Maurice Paul & his Cedar Paul[1] were here—dining on vegetables, there came a War Office envelope to say that Lt. F M Hueffer had been "discharged to duty" on Feb 7th. So he has kept up not writing for 5 weeks nearly & has been back—where?[2] for I do not know for 3 weeks. I told M[aurice] P[aul] that I had "given him the push" he had suggested six months ago & that he had not gone, at least he answers evasively with protestations of affection. The lawyers letter[3] was surely "push" enough. I did not want him to take it, but I should have respected him if he had. The Pauls both argue. Socialism, Pacifism, seem to me "airy" dreams. These people are as unpractical or more so than Shelley. A vague entity or collection of human beings called "The Community" ought, *selon them*, to get & take or be given every place, advantage & commodity. I could not sleep & took my medinal[4] again

Sun., Feb. 25.   My little dialogue—the one I wrote for Somerset Maugham's "*Venture*" was played by "Stockport" Club[5] at the Margaret

[1] Maurice Eden Paul (1865-1944), son of Kegan Paul the publisher, was a physician as well as a writer on social, political, and psychological subjects. He wrote books on *Socialism and Science* (1909), *Karl Marx and Modern Socialism* (1910), and *Psychical Research and Thought Transferance* (1911), and he served as Paris correspondent of the London *Daily Citizen* from 1912 to 1914. His wife Cedar (née Gertrude Mary Davenport) was an opera singer; she collaborated with her husband in translating medical, scientific, and political works.

[2] The lawyer's letter Hunt refers to was one she had Dollymore, her solicitor, send to Ford in July of 1916 withdrawing her financial guarantee to him.

[3] Ford's Service Record indicates that he was at Rouen from February 3 to 24, 1917.

[4] Medinal is the sedative and hypnotic, barbital sodium.

[5] Hunt's dialogue "The Gem and its Setting" appeared in 1903 in Somerset Maugham's short-lived literary magazine, *The Venture*. Maugham was an old friend, confidant, and briefly in 1907 lover of Hunt's. The dialogue depicts the fidelity of the patient, long-suffering suitor, James Knight (played on stage by Fisher White), who is eventually accepted by the heroine. Knight is evidently modelled on Dr. Cholmely, who courted Hunt unsuccessfully but persistently for many years. In her 1936 diary, Hunt looks back on their relationship and justifies her rejection of Cholmely: "I did not ask him to love me and if I had given in it would have killed him since I *hated* his touch." The Stockport Club was a new dramatic society, which gave its first performance on January 30, 1917.

43

Morris Theatre. I took Ethel Mayne.[6] My "Gem & its Setting" played better than I expected. The man who played poor Cholmely! was good. I thanked Fisher White[7] afterwards. Then I went to see Dorothy Coningsby Clarke & her baby & Marguerite Hall,[8] given over to spiritualism since the death of "Ladye" (Mrs Batten).[9] She is permeated with a cold selfishness. It amuses me to see my "Miss Agate" [VH: see "The Doll"][10] turned so contrairy. Isabel Agate wld never have been a spiritualist. But *she* married and Marguerite has refused Thesiger.[11] I supped at the Sir Theodore Cooks[12] & a real German (her nephew) saw me into 49 bus & begged me to speak low because of the policemen who were listening

Mon., Feb. 26.   To Fitzroy Square to buy Bantam tea. Eleanor Jackson to lunch at Kardomah Café. I was very sad. She was sad & preoccupied, trying to disillusion me about F telling me of all his inclinations to all my female friends (well favoured) attempted kissings & so on! She had to spend the afternoon at S Lodge to put me back in my *assiette* again. Ford is certainly a *crétin* of genius. Not one single gentleman's impulse, only

6 Ethel Colburn Mayne (187?-1941) was a novelist, short-story writer, translator, and biographer of Byron. One of Hunt's oldest and most loyal friends, she was asked by Hunt to be executor of her estate, but Mayne died a year before her friend.

7 For Cholmely and White see note 4.

8 Dorothy Coningsby Clarke was a cousin of Marguerite (Radclyffe) Hall (1886-1943) and wife of the composer Robert Coningsby Clarke. Marguerite was an old friend of Hunt's, long before she attracted public notoriety as the author of her novel of lesbianism, *The Well of Loneliness* (1928). In her 1907 diary Hunt describes Hall as "a stately intent sort of body her poetry is her only sex outlet." Though Hunt had declined Hall's amorous advances as early as 1906, when her friend's controversial novel was banned by the police, Hunt was one of the first to decry its suppression.

9 "Ladye" was Mabel Batten, a well-known opera singer and beauty, married to George Batten, Secretary to the Viceroy of India. In 1907 she outraged London society by leaving Batten to move in with Hall, with whom she remained until her death in 1916. Feeling grief and guilt after Ladye's death, Hall turned to spiritualism in an attempt to reach her in the beyond.

10 Violet Hunt's novel *The Doll* (1911) contains a sympathetic portrait of young Isabel Agate, a straightforward and determined heroine ("The whole of her philosophy was summed up in the word 'straight'" [p. 197]), upper-class and head-long, who resembles Marguerite Hall.

11 Ernest Thesiger was a young actor known for his ability at female impersonation.

12 Sir Theodore Cook (1867-1928) was a journalist and editor of the *Field*. Apparently Hunt and Cook's nephew were speaking low because they were speaking German at a time when anti-German sentiment was running high in England.

savage, secret furtive animal ones. Dined at Mrs Stafford's, Valerie Marley's mother. How funny! Valerie phoned me the other morning from an hotel bed, "am in a man's arms, without a stitch on." The voice had a queer conscious ring. "I'm with you!" I said . . .

Tues., Feb. 27.　To the Hydro, Richmond.[13] Dr. Metcalf says I am still very low—my pulse. It is odd to sit in that room with virgins & otherwise, disrobing. One feels like a Prussian, officers & nuns making ready to be raped. The women talk so, even in a temp of 100 degrees. To Mrs Scorer's—& back by bus with Mrs Dummett—women talk: only of Devonport[14] and the restrictions on Paris goods. How ugly dress will be for the time. Dined at Treviglio's with Marguerite Hall, talking of Lodge & Spiritualism.[15] I am a great gun because I knew F Myers.[16] Then of Ford, his genius—his waywardness—his vanity.

Wed., Feb. 28.　F writes to say that he has got his second star[17] & his address—gone "up to the line"—"mine as always." Tea at Mrs Dummett's. I *won't* give Ford's news. Mrs Crawley phoned & told me that I.B.D. means Infantry Base Depot. So apparently F is *not* near the line. I am much happier. Byles[18] dined. At 11, to a "rag"[19] at Tessy Ash-

---

[13] Both Ford and Hunt frequented hydropathic establishments for water therapy. Richmond is about ten miles from London on the north bank of the Thames.

[14] Hudson Ewbanke Kearley, Lord Devonport (1856-1934) founded the International Stores, served as a liberal MP 1892-1910, and as the first food controller 1916-17. On February 26, 1917, he made a speech about the wartime restrictions on imports, warning people against the speculative buying and cornering of food supplies.

[15] Sir Oliver Lodge (1851-1940) was a distinguished physicist and pioneer of wireless telegraphy. His book on psychical research, *Raymond* (1911), was written in response to the death of his son.

[16] F[rederic] W[illiam] H[enry] Myers (1843-1901), poet and essayist, was one of the founders of the Society for Psychical Research and a friend of the Hunt family. In her 1889 diary Violet notes that Myers sent the Hunts tickets for a meeting of the society. Violet never seems to have had much sympathy for psychical research, lamenting to see "a clever, reasonable, earnest man like that wasting his time in addressing such moon struck idiots."

[17] Each bronze service star signifies membership in a unit that participated in a battle or campaign.

[18] Former business manager of *The Throne*, René Byles later served as managing director of Alston Rivers, Ford's publisher, and he remained a loyal friend, apparently closer to Hunt than to Ford during this period. Ford affectionately described him as a "small, grim, bronzed Sheffield man of the wildest prejudices [who] aspired to be the absolute commonsense Englishman" (*South Lodge*, p. 59). Ford also claimed that but for Byles he would often have made one of his threatened "farewells to literature."

[19] In Ford's *Some Do Not . . .*, Valentine Wannop and her brother Edward attend a rag-time party in the same year, 1917.

45

worth's. Thesiger & young Evan Morgan[20] (Lord Tredegar's son & heir) made great fun. Nora Haselden came up & gave me a lesson in fox trotting. She beams on me since I no longer mention Ford. That I hear is the reason she—and Jane (Wells)[21]—avoid my society. Two o'clock home.

Thurs., Mar. 1.   To Selsey with Mrs Apperley, broken pipes etc, our mission. The cottage at Selsey[22] I "hate with the hate of hell—yet I love it passing well." It was the cradle of my love & my discomfiture.

Fri., Mar. 2.   Rain—& paying bills . . . Mrs A[pperley] tells me Sextus Masterman[23] told her F was disliked by his fellow officers because he patronises & lectures them & then is seen coming out of the house of ill fame (at Rouen) himself. But now he has "got his second star." She supposes he is behaving better. I.B.D. means, Mrs Crawley says, Infantry Base Depot: an inglorious role which relieves me of the need of writing to relieve my own feelings. I begin to hope I have none.

Sat., Mar. 3.   Home. To Ethel Mayne's in the evening. She, Irish, abuses us—i e England

Sun., Mar. 4.   Tea with Mrs Marley & her little sweet silly sister who has had two operations & is to have another on Wednesday. The submarine in the Clyde[24] story is authentic. Valerie hears it from Rigg her lover in the Admiralty *after* the event. It sank on trial & did not rise again. The captain got himself shot out, as a torpedo! & was able thus to save 40 men out of 60. The S is still submerged but will be got up. Dined with Fergusons. I find Rose has kept the adoring letters[25] I wrote her when a

20 Lord Tredegar's son, Evan Morgan (b. 1893), served as a member of the Welch Guards during World War I and was known as a poet, writer, and artist.

21 Jane Wells, née Amy Catherine Robbins (1872-1927), was H. G. Wells's second wife. She and Hunt were never close friends, particularly since Hunt had carried on a flirtation with H.G. some ten years before the period of this diary.

22 Hunt rented the Knap, a seaside cottage at Selsey in Sussex, from Edward Heron-Allen (see note 120). The cottage became the center of lively weekend parties with Ford and other friends whom they entertained there.

23 Sextus Masterman served as an officer in Ford's regiment. His older brother Charles was the brilliant liberal statesman, editor of the *Daily News*, and contributor to the *Nation* and the *Athenaeum*. A close friend of Ford's, Charles accompanied Ford and Hunt to Germany in 1913.

24 The Clyde refers to the River Clyde, though possibly to the shipyards as well.

25 Rose (née Cumberbatch) Ferguson was an old friend of Hunt's. Hunt did indeed keep her letters (1879-1925), and they are now in the Ford collection at the Cornell University Library.

schoolgirl. . . . I am not well. It is this life. I am nothing to anybody. Ford is seen coming out of houses of ill fame at Rouen. Miss Ross[26] (the girl in Wales he has I am told) might have something to say to that. Not I— any more. The void is awful. Ford does not think there is one. He thinks that when the war is over, the pieces will be picked up! He *means* to poor dear! And the Gilbert Cannan—Barrie menage[27] has given out. Mrs Buchanan, as Ford used to call her, has bolted & left him to his servant girl & her coming baby. And he has another love now "a Southern" girl. His letters to Mary are like F's to me. She is the one woman, the real one—all the others are merely "illusions." It is a prick for me. I *can't*, but people think our alliance has, too, gone the way of all (younger) flesh!

Mon., Mar. 5. Mrs Pitt Lewis[28] suddenly sent for me to sit with her. I generally go in the evening. She says I am lucky to have my man (if I love him) however faithless, not in the firing line. Her son is. There is something in that, indeed if it wasn't for that, I couldn't hold out. Aunt Amy[29] looks very old. She is. Silvia[30] always talks of me. I said how odd! when she hates me. Aunt Amy said with a funny Hunt gesture, Perhaps it is I who insist on talking of you to her! She told me—she said "I ought not—not even to you." Your grandfather[31] painted many ways and styles. He was a drawing master after all. Once a friend sent for him to see a Gerard Dou[32] he had acquired. It was one of my grandfather's own that

26 Ford's biographies do not mention Miss Ross, but Mizener speculates that Ford had "some kind of sentimental experience" while he was stationed at Cardiff Castle.

27 Gilbert Cannan (1884-1955) was a novelist, translator, and critic, the author of *Round the Corner*, a *succès de scandale*, suppressed by the censor for its frankness. He married the actress Mary Ansell, former wife of J. M. Barrie the playwright. That marriage lasted only a few years, and Cannan was certified insane in 1919. In an undated entry in her papers, Hunt recalls Cannan, tired of his wife, saying that women should leave open the cage door: "I said yes but you would expect her to stay in the cage herself and *that* I wouldn't do! And yet I was doing it all the time, leaving the door open for Ford to fly to Brigit."

28 Mrs. Pitt Lewis was a Hunt family friend, the wife of George Pitt Lewis, a distinguished lawyer.

29 Aunt Amy was the sister of Hunt's father, the artist Alfred Hunt (1830-1896).

30 Silvia Kingsley Fogg-Elliot was Violet's youngest sister; she and another sister, Venice, quarreled with Violet over the disposition of their mother's will.

31 Violet's grandfather, Andrew Hunt (1790-1861), was also an artist and an early member of the Liverpool Academy of Arts.

32 Gerard Dou (1613-1675), one of Rembrandt's first pupils, painted history and genre scenes as well as portraits.

had somehow or other got on to the market. Aunt A says grandpapa & grandma sat up all night talking it over. Should they undeceive the owner? They decided not. Ethel Mayne came in the evening & I read my 1st part done *"The Perpetual Bridesmaid"* to her. She said it was very amusing: quite in my old vulgar sparkling manner—unworthy of me in fact. So Ford gets justified. For he had worked me out of it[,] tried to.

Tues., Mar. 6.   I had a woman in to massage my hair. It is so thin & undo-able now, that all the loose hairs are taken out of it by I daresay more healthy. To Ezra Pound's.[33] They talk only of Joyce's book.[34]

Wed., Mar. 7.   Dining with a convinced Irish Pacifist—dined off fish, game & trifle! "We don't mind: we are not English." And abuse of Grey[35] who caused the War by his isolation (attempted) of Germany. I saw Mrs Luivend [?] too today ill in bed, an abcess in her chest a fathom deep unhealed. Poor old maid. She says, "Aren't you going to get rid of F? It was all wrong—from the beginning dear. Taking another woman's husband!"

Thurs., Mar. 8.   A letter from F dated yesterday. The YMCA at Grosvenor Gardens. He "advises" Dear V, that he is in town on duty for 3 days —may get an extra but doesn't know. Is mine FMH. 2:45. Made chair covers. It is snowing. Out all day—20 to 12 home. All silent. No word from F—my death warrant. I must do it! But I shan't be able to stand it.

---

33 Ezra Pound (1885-1972), a loyal friend of both Hunt and Ford, often visited Hunt's house, South Lodge, and led the tennis parties headquartered there. Later in a letter he wrote of Hunt, "glad of confirmation re/ V's virchoos, alZO the number and quality of her friends OUGHT by any logik prozess to prove she warnt totally 'that VIper'" (Mizener, p. 239). Pound considered himself Ford's champion, praising his "vision of perfection" in a 1914 review of Ford's *Collected Poems*.

34 The work of Joyce's that everyone is talking about is *A Portrait of the Artist as a Young Man*, published as a book in England for the first time in 1916, although it had appeared serially in Pound's journal *The Egoist* in 1914 and 1915. Pound eloquently defended Joyce against charges of smuttiness, persuading Harriet Weaver to handle *Portrait*'s English issue and trying to get his own publisher Marshall to put out its American edition.

35 Edward Grey, first Viscount of Falloden (1862-1933), served in the House of Commons from 1885 to 1916 as liberal representative for Berwick-on-Tweed and as Secretary of State for foreign affairs. On August 3, 1914, he made the historic speech in the House of Commons giving Great Britain's reasons for entering World War I. Ford told Edgar Jepson that on the previous day he had spent the morning with Prime Minister Asquith and Grey, who reiterated before him the question, "Shall we fight, Hueffer, or shall we not fight?"

Fri., Mar. 9. *Could* not stand it. Lucy Masterman[36] said at 6 I ought to let him know I was willing to see him—if I wanted not to lose my hold over him—as the lawyer's letter was prohibitive. I thought over it and Mrs Crawley, where I dined, gave me such a stiff cocktail & there was champagne at dinner that I was so drunk that on my way back via Portland Road, I telephoned to the YMCA. The nurse there said that Hueffer was out but she'd give a message, & sure enough he phoned. "Did I wish to speak to him?" I said "I would see him." He said "It is in your hands," & I replied, "I know." We made an appt. to meet at the London Lib. at 12. We did. I don't believe he has got a second star? It is not on. We lunched. to see Mrs Keary tea at Mrs Crawleys. Theatre. *Bing Boys.*[37] *C'etait écoeurant.* Then he *would* see me home and we had an explanation. He says if he wrote a love letter to Miss Ross it was in delirium & intended for Brigit[38] with whom he is still infatuated, and who wrote to him at Cap Martin.[39] He says he must go to her if she sends for him but that she won't. He'll give up the others—& write to no woman at all! So it was a miserable climb down. It was 2 in the morning & he suggested my putting him up. I did. [VH: But did we? 1936 V asks]

Sun., Mar. 11.   Ford lunched with a man at Authors Club:[40] I with Mrs Marley, fetched at 3:30 & to the Haynes.[41] Rebecca West[42] was

---

[36] Lucy Masterman, Charles's wife, appears to have acted as mediator in the Ford-Hunt relationship, since at the end of 1917 Ford inquired of her if she could find him cheap lodgings in London, South Lodge apparently being unavailable to him.

[37] Hunt would have seen at the London Opera House *The Other Bing Boys: A Picture of London Life*, a sequel to the popular revue, *The Bing Boys are Here*, which had closed in January.

[38] Brigit Patmore was a red-haired Irish beauty twenty years younger than Hunt, the wife of a successful insurance broker, Deighton, the grandson of Coventry Patmore. In her effort to re-establish her family's Pre-Raphaelite connections, Hunt called on the Patmores and she and Brigit became fast friends. Ford developed an infatuation for Brigit and Hunt suspected an affair between them, probably with good reason. In later years, however, Brigit denied any attraction to Ford and her sympathies remained with Hunt. After being introduced by Violet to Pound, Brigit entered the circle of the Imagists and in the late 1920s lived with Richard Aldington.

[39] Cap Martin, at Menton in France, was the site of a Red Cross Hotel, to which Army doctors had sent Ford at the end of December, 1916. Ford left Cap Martin on February 2, 1917, for Rouen.

[40] The Authors Club, at 3 Whitehall Court, was founded by Walter Besant, and by 1914 it had become a comfortable gathering place for professional writers.

[41] E. S. P. Haynes was a staff member of Cecil Chesterton's weekly, *The New Witness* and a friend and supporter of Ford's.

there & the author of *"Limehouse Nights"*[43] who fainted—tipsy—in the W C. Then home. He made me a scene about Byles & Dolleymore & Sims[44]—his friend, my lawyer & another friend. Any stick to beat a (female) dog with—said that he would go out of the house tomorrow & not reënter it unless I promised to drop them. I refused. We went to the W L Georges[45] and there was Gwen Otter[46] & Baroness Von Hutten.[47] Then he made an excuse to stop tonight but I was ready for him & had his room prepared. We parted downstairs coldly

Mon., Mar. 12.   It went well. I slept. He did. He is very ill I think. I

---

[42] Rebecca West (1892-1983), the distinguished novelist, critic, and journalist, entered Hunt's life in about 1912 and remained a close friend both during her own affair with H. G. Wells, when Hunt was practically her only confidante, and during Hunt's affair with Ford, when their roles were reversed. They were mutually supportive while incurring public outrage: Hunt called West, in a letter to Wells, "the sweetest person one could have about a house" (Gordon N. Ray, *H. G. Wells and Rebecca West* [New Haven: Yale University Press, 1974], p. 57). And West comforted Hunt during her bitter family quarrels: "Cheer up! The only people who are really well treated by life are people like Mrs H[umphry] Ward and Mrs J[oseph] C[onrad] . . . and that's too heavy a price to pay" (*I Have This to Say*, p. 110).

[43] The author of *Limehouse Nights: Tales of Chinatown* (London: Grant Richards, 1916) was Thomas Burke (1887-1945).

[44] Kenneth Dolleymore was Hunt's lawyer, a solicitor for the firm of Richardson, Sadler, and Co. Sims may have been Ernest F. Sims, a member of the 3rd Welch Regiment, from whom Hunt gathered information about Ford. In 1916 Sims wrote to Hunt: "I saw your husband at a cricket match yesterday—he was not playing but was looking very fit & well, not in the least overworked, and was very busy looking after the female guests" (Cornell University Library). Several years later, Ford accused Hunt of talking about him indiscreetly, implying that he lived off her and fueling gossip about his German connections. He wrote his mother that he told Violet he would break with her for good unless she gave up her relationship with "these three gentlemen," perhaps Byles, Dolleymore, and Sims.

[45] W[alter] L[ionel] George (1882-1926), a French-born novelist who lived and wrote in England, was known for his liberal, pacifist, and feminist sympathies as well as for his unconventional life. Hunt speaks affectionately of him as "the fast friend through thick and thin of myself and Joseph Leopold [Ford]" (*I Have This to Say*, p. 215).

[46] Gwen Otter was a long-time friend of Hunt's and a popular London hostess at her flat in Cheyne Court. Her parties were known for their fine food, notable guests, and lively conversation.

[47] American-born Baroness Von Hutten (1874-1957) achieved instant success as an author with her first novel *Pam* (1905). Originally Bettina Riddle of Pennsylvania, she married Freiherr Von Hutten zum Stolzenberg of Bavaria in 1897. They were divorced in 1909, after which she lived alternately in England and America.

begin to believe in the "gassing,"[48] and he has said nothing about B & D & S.

Tues., Mar. 13.   Scenes. door shut.

Wed., Mar. 14.   Dined Crawleys. To Selsey. He asked a Mr West of the Welch to come down for weekend. I agreed. We were alone in the house and that spasm of regret, of sexual rage overcame me. I went to his room & said I was lonely. We argued. He returned to the Dolleymore letter, and that he had quite made up his mind that all was over & had only written to notify his arrival to give me a chance of reconsidering my decision *not* to cast off the three. Then he became abusive & asked me not to speak in a whining voice, like the creaking of a door! . . . . I said "Well let us settle it . . . are you in love with Brigit?" "Of course I am!" he retorted. What else cld a churl like him have said? And F went away from the room. I made yet another attempt . . . and the result that I went to his bed & lay alone & cold for 2 minutes. Then went back to my own.

Thurs., Mar. 15.   Mrs Apperley came down & Ford spent most of the time helping her with her house. We don't meet after saying Goodnight again.

Fri., Mar. 16.   The same

Sat., Mar. 17.   Mr West (3rd Welch) came & Bridge

Sun., Mar. 18.   ibid

Mon., Mar. 19.   I got a "scunner" of staying with F & came up with W[est] & Apperley. Dined Byles.

Tues., Mar. 20.   Dined West

Wed., Mar. 21.   Returned Selsey. F did not meet me, but *bonafide* expected me. No *rapprochement*

Thurs., Mar. 22.   It was an historic evening. Something changed. I sat on his knee & he *débité* extraordinary fatuities—so much so that he stopped & in the midst of my silence said, "I may seem very fatuous . . . ." I did not deny it but lay with my head on his shoulder . . . . my unusual silence & lack of combativeness brought it out. And these are some of the

---

[48] In 1916 Ford wrote to his younger daughter that "the gas of the Huns has pretty well done for my lungs" (*The Last Pre-Raphaelite*, p. 197), but Mizener unequivocally asserts that Ford was never wounded or gassed.

51

things he said: "I will give you my reasons (for my not loving you but B[rigit]) if you ask for them . . . I would not be here if I didn't care for you . . . . but I shld be at Brighton (where she was) . . . I do love you, I dare say, with the reservation that in a still small room B is sitting waiting for me & if she sends for me, I will go to her. I must . . . . There may be no one in the quiet room—you, in fact but you never *were* quiet. You never were kind to me like these other women. You were—are—stimulating if you like. B means to me quiet appreciation—praise . . . encouragement . . . . you never praised me—never once!" And then again he began: "I don't think you realise what I have seen & been" etc & then began the tedious self laudation of the British officer, the resentment against so called civilian indifference, the complaint that he is not treated as a wounded hero . . . ad lib—or ad nauseam. He looked at me curiously . . . . "You know dear, I am not the sort of animal that makes love to women. I never shall, again. I don't care about women, really. I am cold and I have one passion now, the Army & that England should win . . . I believe I wld sacrifice *even* Brigit to the army! I am a broken down man." *Next breath* "I am a man, fit, strong—gallant, not the shivering pill-taking valetudinarian you took . . . . Why don't you go in for the line in which you appeal to me—always did. I admire you, for your intellect —no not your intellect but character & personality—but no, you never waked in me the feeling you speak of . . . . Good god, my dear, take what you can get, like other women. If you want me to take your hand: put out yours—if you want to attract me be attractive. It's the lot of all women!"

Talking of Brigit's letter to him written from her death bed to his (supposed to be) he said that it was the *only* thing she *could* do, that she had treated him very improperly. "I assure you the receipt of her letter made me very happy. I was a different man from the moment."

I said "Brigit was wicked. If I can hurt her I will. I wish she had died!" Then he hugged me & smiled:

"There now—that is the first, human—natural thing you have said! I suppose it will all settle itself. You & Brigit will claw each other & either she will get me—or you. That's life. Take what you can get."

I said "I don't believe in Brigit. You used her to cover your retreat from the flirtation with a second rate garrison hack like Miss Ross. It sounded better—an undying passion for a married woman with 2 boys & half her inside cut away" . . . "My dear you're too clever by half, that's the matter with you."

52

"Don't be a silly woman . . . come to my bed if you will . . . ."

I went & stayed a moment. He embraced me dully—then slept . . . I began to go away. "What are you doing? Can't you stay here?" "No. I can't sleep . . . . you just bore me." "That's that!" he said

Fri., Mar. 23.   To town. Very cold. He came & lay in my bed & I left it.

Sun., Mar. 25.   Mr West & Mrs C. Clarke lunched. Supped alone & played cards

Mon., Mar. 26.   I saw Byles. Dined Bellottis with the Ezra Pound crowd[49]

Tues., Mar. 27.   Dined at home. Cards.

Wed., Mar. 28.   F went to the Haseldens for Bridge. I could not stand it. I told him I wanted him to go—& not sleep here if he didn't love me. He said he cared for me but he wouldn't be bound—the feeling of the moment. He explained—that I was a most irritating person to live with— that he couldn't love me in this house with these old servants . . . . that domesticity had killed the feeling . . . . I said that in that case I wanted him to go out of this house & sleep away from me . . . . He said he'd go— but reluctantly . . . . this afternoon. I said no—*now*, before lunch—for good. He said "All right" & went & then came back . . . . Would I send his things on or make a parcel? . . . etc. I was so blind with rage I said nothing. Then he began to fulminate . . . . the house, S Lodge, was above his means. He was a pauper . . . it was half his—he had a *right* to a room in it![50] Astounding statements! Does he believe them? He went on that I had trumped him about & had by insulting a servant of the King had insulted the British Army. The 3 days at the YMCA still rankled and I had to give in . . .

He went out about 3—he said Shall I come in when I come back from

---

[49] "While Hueffer and others were at the front, a certain amount of bohemian life went on in London. During the latter part of the conflict, weekly dinners were held at Bellotti's in Soho. Old-timers like Pound, Eliot, Lewis, Violet Hunt, H.D., Harriet Weaver, and occasionally Hueffer or Aldington, had brought into their circle some new members: Mary Butts, for instance, who wanted to be a social worker and a writer, and Stella Bowen, a young Australian painter, for whom Ezra Pound organized parties." (Bernard Poli, *Ford and the Transatlantic Review* [Syracuse: Syracuse University Press, 1967], pp. 7-8.)

[50] Early in 1910, when Ford was serving a ten-day jail sentence for non-support of his wife Elsie, Hunt and Elsie's sister Mary Martindale dismantled his 84 Holland Park Avenue apartment and moved his things into South Lodge, where he lived with Hunt and her mother, ostensibly as a boarder, paying £3 a week.

Nora's & say Goodnight? I said "No not anything unless you love me."
He made a slight sound of negation & went. Then I saw red. I phoned
to Metcalfs & got a room & at 9, I went up there to Richmond.

Thurs., Mar. 29.   I phoned F to say I was coming back to luncheon.
He is going to golf with Nora Haselden. He hasn't turned a hair. Got
home to lunch. At tea at Mrs Pitt L[ewis]. Child[51] rang me up. F had
phoned he was going—at night & to get his clothes & things ready. He
turned up at 6:30, said he was ordered to report at Rhyl & go to France
on Tuesday—an obvious untruth.[52] He said the order was in the paper.
It wasn't. I looked. He handed it to me. A scene—at dinner. He said "I
go at midnight, or I can stay till next day—if you ask me to." What
could I say but that I didn't want him to stay unless—the red rag! But
he wanted to go to Mrs Rooks—& go he did. He had accused me,
apropos of my demands for love of having "a bed room mind." Then at
night he said "Shall I come & sleep with you." I said "yes if you like."
He lay like a log & groused—groused blue & deep. He *is* awfully disappointed & unhappy & needy. He never kissed me—one of those awful
lie-a-beds when one lies & thinks & wonders when the other person is
going to speak

Fri., Mar. 30.   Another row at breakfast. I phoned Mrs Macdonald that
we were not coming & she said "how horrid for you—how sad to lose
him!" and as she knows all about it, I added, "It's not an unmitigated
evil .... things have been very horrid ...."
   Ford heard. He came & said so. He repeated ad nauseam the "I don't
love you" .... The *you have ruined me!* touch ... & I was fairly cor-
nered. I let out He was stubborn .... I offered to have no confidante at
all if he wld be mine—mine as before. He said he could not. He could
promise nothing! He was rampant. I had lost all. I gave in. I went to
Euston with him via Authors Club & Bank—£11 overdrawn. That
seemed to finish him. At Euston was Ferris Greenslet[53] *en retour* to America—Crewe.[54] Liverpool. It made the parting easier. F was a *little*—very

51 Annie Child was Hunt's long-time parlormaid and her only companion in her
   lonely final years.
52 After being invalided during March, Ford was at the beginning of April given
   light duty as captain of a company of the 23 King's Liverpool Regiment at Kinmel
   Park. Rhyl is in North Wales.
53 Ferris Greenslet (1875-1959) was a friend of Ford's, a writer himself, associate
   editor of the *Atlantic* from 1903 to 1907, and literary editor for Houghton Mifflin
   from 1908 to 1942.
54 Crewe is an important railway junction on the way to Liverpool.

little—melted. He murmured "Wait & see what happens." I said "I will be very glad if you come back to S Lodge even if you *don't* love me." He replied "That is nice of you, dear." I saw Byles, who is pessimistic of all but a "state of polite indifference" on both sides. At 6 Mrs ——— [sic] rang me up said Sextus (one of Fs COs) was here, & said, on hearing that F had gone back to Wales:—"Then he's done for, he'll find his order to relinquish waiting for him!" Malice, or truth. I have heard rumours of it before from another source. Gilbert West, a soldier, & Barbara Stratton dined. I wrote a nice empty letter to F.

Sat., Mar. 31. To tea with Mrs Marley in her own house, & to Ethel Mayne who always speaks up for Ford.

Sun., Apr. 1. I hear Sextus—perfectly friendly—yet he said that if Ford went back to Wales he was done for. The letter ordering him to relinquish C—[commission] was awaiting him there. Is it an April jest?

Mon., Apr. 2. Ford wrote coldly, fatuously, evasively as he always will write . . . Dined Bellottis with Mrs West . . . Have written Ford.

Tues., Apr. 3. To Selsey with Child. It's awful: the *saudades*.[55]

Wed., Apr. 4. Mrs W L George came—pretty empty sympathetic kind. And Ford writes—coldly—a letter that he wld not have written even to Mary Martindale[56] in the old days. He has to go before a medical board . . . hedging!

Thurs., Apr. 5. F again. Med. B. won't pass him for France. Hedging again! Oh what is the good of my life, hanging *in ribbons* round a man who does not care for me!

Fri., Apr. 6 (Good). W L George came. He gave me good advice. He walked me on the sea shore

Sat., Apr. 7. George's advice "Reduce F." "He has *la folie des gran-deurs*." Go away. Take a flat. Let S Lodge . . . *et patati—et fatata*! All impossible to a woman like me! I can't hold out against loneliness, &

---

[55] *Saudades*: a Portuguese term suggesting nostalgia or a longing for something absent.

[56] Mary Martindale, Elsie Martindale Hueffer's mentally unstable older sister, nurtured a passion for Ford; she even carried on an affair with him while he was married to Elsie. By the time Hunt had supplanted Elsie, Mary had become Hunt's friend, lending respectability to the establishment at South Lodge by briefly living with them.

neglect. Besides, there's no time. "For at my heels I always Time...
chariots hurrying near."

Sun., Apr. 8.   More talk.

Mon., Apr. 9.   do. G left

Tues., Apr. 10.   She left. And I stay & try to cultivate repose....

Wed., Apr. 11.   Sextus can't understand F's affairs. He knows... things
& he guesses & he tells things & takes them back. He is disappointed in
F. He makes a rotten soldier.[57] Fool Sextus to have hoped otherwise. The
Apperleys dined.

Thurs., Apr. 12.   The Tarbutt is going to take The Knap for a fortnight. The other people come in in May. I am better but so lonely. I
began the sequel to *Their Lives*[58] & did some good work. I shall finish
the 1st chapter fair & send it to Ford. His wall flower from Denbigh
against my violets from Selsey. Isn't it funny—our tossing flowers to each
other across chaos! But he does not know it is chaos. Does he know
anything, in his triple case of egotism?

Fri., Apr. 13.   Mrs Apperley asked Child & me to stay on with them till
they go. So we are going to. The burst of sunlight on Child's face showed
me what to say. She is kinder to me than Ford... But I must come to
see that I have not been so very good to Ford that he must be eternally
grateful. He paid as he went along: in caresses. And now I can no longer
subvenir to his wants: give him pleasurable sensations of opulence of

---

[57] In August 1916, Colonel Cooke wrote a letter to the headquarters of the 58th
Brigade: "I consider that he is quite unsuitable to perform the duties required of
an officer in this campaign. He would not inspire his men with confidence and
his power as a leader is nil.... I recommend that he be sent home as early as
possible as there is no use to which I can put him. I could not place him in
command of men in the field. I cannot recommend him for employment at home"
(Mizener, p. 572). Ford denied Cooke's charges and cherished the ideal of military
competence. In *Parade's End* he depicts the heroic Christopher Tietjens, who
resembles himself in many ways, as an unjustly maligned soldier.

[58] Violet Hunt's novel, *Their Lives*, was published in 1918 by Stanley Paul and its
sequel, *Their Hearts*, appeared in 1921. The novels depict the strained relationships
between the three growing daughters of an insufficiently appreciated landscape
painter. Ford wrote a laudatory preface to *Their Lives* under the pseudonym Miles
Ignotus. For a discussion of these novels as Pre-Raphaelite autobiographies and
romans à clef, see Robert and Marie Secor, "Lives and Hearts in Pre-Raphaelite
England: The Autobiographical Novels of Violet Hunt," *Pre-Raphaelite Review*,
2, May 1979, pp. 59-70.

flattery of consequence. I am not doing my part & he does not give! me anything at all

Sat., Apr. 14. If I *don't* write: it will be a grievance. *Eh bien!* that even has ceased to frighten me. Time was I would submit to any indignity not to be left out—alone—loose in the empyrean. Now I am just as lost, even though we are friends. I can do without the kind of letter he is able to write to me.

Sun., Apr. 15. Tea with Mrs Tarbutt at The Knap. She has it for a fortnight £2.2 week. She took it for Nell & Percy. Percy won't now let Nell come down—The Knap is contaminated for him by the tenancy of Ford. How maddening they are! [VH: He hated Ford I see. Wisdom of 1936 Ford was jealous]

Mon., Apr. 16. Ford wrote some days ago asking for his tunic his clubs & some copies of his books! He also suggests I shd come to St Asaph's, a boarding house there where he cld ride over to see me on a bike—5 miles—which I should bring!

Wed., Apr. 18. I wrote to Brigit at Slough.

Thurs., Apr. 19. Eleanor Jackson came. She says Nora H thinks F a "good man—a martyr to his pledged word. He says he is to stick to me whatever I do, since the circumstances in which we came together make it impossible for him to leave me." If I were married to him, he would do so without compunction as he did Elsie. So he gives it all away! my poor reputation for an ounce of flattery from Nora Haselden!

Fri., Apr. 20. All day at Byle's house with Brigit & Deighton. She is as sweet as ever. Young looking hair dyed, weak & ill, no personality. That is her charm for F. She says he must always pose—never real—histrionic to his fingertips . . . Dreaming—*not* dreaming true—false to himself. Deighton is a worm. B doesn't care a pin for F. She succumbed from the flattery of his suit—his plausibility . . . and her motto is O Wilde's: "For each man kills the thing he loves."[59] I wrote to F from here & sent him his clubs

Sat., Apr. 21. E Jackson came. She said, "You've got him of course but not as you want. You'll never get him as you want, unless you alter yourself to suit him & give him money. When he told you to make yourself attractive if you wanted to attract him: he didn't mean dye your hair

[59] The Wilde quotation is from "The Ballad of Reading Gaol," 1898.

or paint or make love—he doesn't care if you look a hundred, so long as you give him money & make S Lodge pleasant!" And that is true, I see. I wrote F the first "non-calculated" letter for a year & a half. I said I observed that his indifference to me had dated from my withdrawal of my *guarantee*[60] in July 1916 . . . I offered to make him an allowance . . . I wished I had no money & was a clerk at 25/ a week like Miss Ross. There will be a row, but I would prefer F to hate me to ignoring me as he is doing.

Sun., Apr. 22.   To the Defries. He took The Knap for Sept. £15.15. Moiseiwitsch & Daisy Kennedy[61] here. Their talk turned to Beethoven. Daisy beautiful & famous, mended her husband's vest in the back room at Chiswick

Mon., Apr. 23.   F wrote & says he has applied to be allowed to relinquish his commission![62] He cannot "stand the merciless financial strain." No one could, he believes.

Tues., Apr. 24.   Wonders. Much happier. The idea of once more chancing a hold on my Frankenstein monster.

Wed., Apr. 25.   Brigit & D came to stay. They took me to the *Bing Girls*.[63] I was amused. I could love B—I suppose if I believed in F & his statements I could not. So—

Thurs., Apr. 26.   They left. F's letter came. I made her read it.
Ford is not poor: £23 to good. So I think his lamentations, & excuse of poverty is his way of letting himself out of the army gracefully. And I am happier—almost happy. For we must, if he is out of the Army either live together or not. To the Bellotti dinner. I sat next Edgar Jep-

---

[60] The withdrawal of the guarantee is the lawyer's letter first mentioned on February 24.

[61] Benno Moiseiwitsch (1890-1963) was a Russian-born pianist, an exponent of the music of the Romantic composers. He first appeared in Britain in 1908. Daisy Kennedy (b. 1893), the Australian-born violinist, made her debut in Vienna and in London in 1911. In 1914 she was married to Moiseiwitsch, but the marriage ended in divorce, and she remarried in 1924 the poet and novelist John Drinkwater.

[62] Instead of resigning, Ford was promoted to lieutenant on July 1, 1917. He relinquished his commission because of ill health on January 7, 1919.

[63] *The Bing Girls are There: A Musical Poster in Eight Folios* was apparently another musical in the Bing Boy series; this one played at the Alhambra Theatre.

son.[64] He has had a letter from F consulting him as to the feasibility of hypothecating his copyrights to the Literary Fund, to enable him to stay in the Army. *Gott bewahre!* But E Jepson wasn't even taken in! He said he hadn't answered: F was much better out! But F won't think so: & if I go on with him, it will be a dog's life—(or a bitch's).

Fri., Apr. 27.   Furious letter from F. He says incidentally that we have one way or another muddled our life: that I certainly am more responsible than he on the sentimental side. That from F who has been unfaithful twice in 2 years! And not blamed, but *choyé* the first time.

Sat., Apr. 28.   Wrote to F via Brigit. Lunched at Mrs Dummett & Reeve Wallace.

Sun., Apr. 29.   F's letter to Edgar Jepson gives address *Capt* F M H. He says he is not allowed to go out to France but has been given a Cy[65] as a sop. Ezra was here all the afternoon & spoke words of *real* wisdom. I expect too much. But still it is a matter of personal liking & I want F in the house so much that I will be his housekeeper in it & nothing more.

Mon., Apr. 30.   He wrote to thank me for the telegram re overdraft. Dined at a new place with Mrs Marley, Molinari's & coffee at Byles.

Tues., May 1.   Byles dined . . . he says F & me—hopeless. I have nothing in the world to do. I want to ask F to come to me at Fordingbridge & hear the nightingales[66] but then I remember I offered to go to Chester and he took no notice. One is proud—what's the good, but one is. And in fits one isn't, & it seems as if an embrace was enough. "I don't like the word embrace" as F remarked. I read Brigit's letter to Byles, the one where she says I am "the eternal Pilgrim of love."

---

[64] Edgar Jepson (1863-1938) was a popular and prolific novelist, the author of many romantic tales of adventure and a number of stories about children. A frequent mediator between Ford and Hunt, he is best remembered for his two autobiographical works, *Memories of a Victorian* (1933) and *Memories of an Edwardian* (1937).

[65] Ford received his captaincy on January 7, 1918.

[66] Fordingbridge, Hampshire, where Hunt spent some happier times with Ford. She wrote in *The Flurried Years*, "At Fordingbridge I heard, for the first time, the crude, harsh shout of the nightingale, for all the world like the wail of a beggar's baby abandoned under a hedge. I told the naturalist [W. H. Hudson] about that long afterwards, and he related to me the story of Procne and the slain child, saying that what I had heard was surely the cry of Philomela: 'Swallow, my sister, oh sister swallow . . .'" (p. 101).

Wed., May 2. My first infidelity to F.[67]

Thurs., May 3. The War Bread makes me ill. F writes vaguely, rudely for money! It must be so. He is in such another crisis as that which brought him to me in 1909,[68] and this time I am not rich. Mrs Braine of Cardiff rang up & came, I fancied to get me to give up F's letter to Miss Ross—But no: she is *not* Miss R's confidante and by assuming, on Ford's word, that it was so, I have done the poor girl a very bad turn. She is going to be *strafed* for conducting an intrigue with a married man under her, Mrs Braine's, roof! F's fault. I gave D Batten some seeding potatoes to plant . . . 6. We have made a row & some lettuces.

Fri., May 4. To the W L Georges. If Child is to keep F around the house like a novel by H James[69] F & I may be lovers again! A joke. I could but nothing else. He probably can't but anything else!

Sun., May 6. To DeLaras concert[70] with V. V. Marley. Her man dined. Navy. The Duchess of Rutland (Phryne from old) . . . was there . . . such a masque of *plâtre* such fine lines. Such a queer 1880 face—our ideal beauty in those days.

Mon., May 7. Tea Juliet Soskice.[71] She wants me to let Ford do alone, for his good . . . He wouldn't even if I would. I wrote, just a line to say my not writing was not meant unkindly—a leaf out of his book. I am dreadfully weak & sad. A kind letter from Jane [Wells]. Ford lied: she was not even at that dinner at Kelton's that night. I wrote to Ford. I said I would write if my letters would do him any good. I wanted to try to tell him how he was forcing me into an economic relation I could not fulfill, that I knew I never said. Byles dined.

[67] Not ascertained.

[68] In June 1909, *The English Review* was in financial difficulty and Ford was depressed about its and his own future. Hunt claims that she came to his lodgings at Holland Park Avenue and rescued him from suicide at this time, confiscating from him a bottle marked "Poison."

[69] The Henry James novel Hunt refers to could be either *The Awkward Age* or *What Maisie Knew*, where Maisie is frequently kept "around the house" to lend respectability to the affair of Sir Claude and Mrs. Beale.

[70] Mrs. Isidore DeLara directed a concert of French music as a war benefit, sponsored by the French Minister of Fine Arts.

[71] Juliet Soskice was Ford's sister, herself a writer, composer, and translator from the Russian. In 1917 she published translations of Kryshanovskaya and Nekrasov. She married David Soskice, a Russian emigré.

Tues., May 8.   I sent a telegram to F to say that I had a chance of selling S. Lodge. Byles plagued me so to do it—to sell it. He says we shall never be able in any circs be happy in this house. I differ. I am too materialistic, F too thick skinned to mind, if other things are equal. . . .

Wed., May 9.   F wired that he thought it would be a pity, but was very uncertain. *Love.* The first time he has used the word to me except in discussion since July 16, 1916. And now in a telegram. He is *impayable.* I remember what he says he wants: problem to find a quiet woman, who will sleep in his arms & ask not so many questions. Then she must be a woman he loves—as I was, when I did. One can, when love is a state, not a mood. But he wants it to be a mood & that precludes wifely quiescence & passivity. I long to be able to tell him that I have not love for him enough and not even respect only an unholy passion that will last till I die, to him . . . . I don't want his mere society—that's love. I want his manifestations [—] that's passion. But whether I get it is another matter. And it is what he asks for when he announces that he doesn't love me beyond the mood of the moment—can't be bound etc. Such a clever man to be so stupid—or is he stupid? As Jesuit priests are stupid.

A week's lapse. Nothing doing.

Mon., May 14.   F wrote—more money talk & covert begging. He begins "I am ashamed not to have answered your letter" . . . details, misery, begging. Then "As far as I am concerned, I intend to return to you at the end of the war wherever you are . . ." More. But I have been in a white heat of fury all day! I spent it out of doors. I wrote early this morning "It is time you left off writing to me as if I were your maiden aunt . . . You say you are ashamed to have been so long writing. There is no obligation for a man to write to his mistress unless he wants to or to return to her after the war unless he wants to very much." And now 11 :30 pm my courage flags. F will punish me for my act of insubordination & I am so very vulnerable . . . Bed & I hope rest. What is to become of me? I am *ballottié* by the caprice of one man—I, a genius as he says. Ruined.

Tues., May 15.   F wrote. To the stores. I already regret my violent note for what good will it do? It won't even pierce his hide of rhinoceros.

Wed., May 16.   Another letter from F. Lamentation about the waste of him. Have they dismissed him? I saw Mrs Jepson. She is a good comfort. And politically Russia is "going to do the dirty on us"![72]

Thurs., May 17. Working. Hair massaged, dined Marley. I feel as if all that kept me to Ford was dead. We shall have to—& shall be unable to—begin again.

Fri., May 18. Wrote Ford, pacific—silly.

Sat., May 19. No letter from F. He *is* a rotten man. It is contemptible to practise on my helpless position—fond of him too & lonely forever because of him to hang me up till the end of war—or till he is chucked & wants a home & a sandbag. I am trying not to get my face distorted with rage. I am going to Rebecca's [West] at Leigh on Sea[73] today

Sun., May 20. Oh the sadness & the wisdom of Rebecca! The boy is like Gyp[74]—spoilt & sad & soft—more like his mother. There was a storm. We thought it was a naval engagement off Canvey Island

Mon., May 21. Home, for an interview with Silvia.
Ethel Redley took me. Silvia's attitude was no, I don't trust you—I did love you—all gone by your conduct your want of straight forwardness. I agree with Venie. You did forge & steal & get false influence over my mother & worse, you were cruel to her.[75] If you would *own* you had done wrong I might forgive & forget, but how can I if you say you did not do wrong. I got so angry at her impossible reasoning I called her a damned little cat . . . She hesitated temporized, said "she must think" & then stiffened again. It is no good.

Thurs., May 24. F wrote, asked for his commission [?] suit of mufti & pass book. Sent them all. It may still be bluff. The Bellotti dinner was nice.

72 Alexander Kerensky was appointed Minister of War for Russia on this date and premier in July of the same year. In September he crushed Kornilov's military revolt, but was deposed by the Bolsheviks in November, when he fled to France.

73 Leigh-on-Sea, in Essex, is where Wells installed West and their son in a charming house with a view of the Thames estuary.

74 Gyp (or Gip) was the nickname of George Philip Wells, born in 1901; he was the older son of H. G. and Jane Wells. The boy Hunt refers to is Anthony West, born August 4, 1914, the son of H. G. Wells and Rebecca West.

75 Hunt bought the lease to South Lodge and lived there, caring for her ailing mother until she died in 1912. The family believed that Violet was squandering her mother's money, and her sisters Silvia and Venice began a series of legal actions, even contesting Mrs. Hunt's will.

Mon., May 28. F asks me if I would care to join him Tuesday at Redcar or Whitby[76]—wired "delighted." We must end this

Tues., May 29. To Whitby. F turned up at 9. Dined & shared my room & we had a row about Miss Ross & what I had done to her about Mrs Braine. We made a horrid noise & people opened their doors at us. A reconciliation. I was drunk.

Wed., May 30. Redcar is the battalion headquarters. F thought Whitby was nearer. We had to go to Redcar, to the Coatham Hotel. He *is* silly

Thurs., May 31. The colonel's wife is easy to nobble.[77] I do. I shall. F is placable & calm & so am I—by effort.

Fri., June 1. He is growing colder. He has toothache adroitly every night at 10—or thereabout. I don't care

Sat., June 2. It goes on. I asked him if at Xmas when he was in hospital he loved Miss Ross, or me—no definite reply. I didn't expect it. I was teasing. The memory of my infidelity [of May 2] bears me up. Then I said "If you were very ill then and the doctor had said that someone shld be sent for would you have sent for me?" He was "on his ear" in a moment. "It depends—one can't tell at supreme moments. I might have sent for you or Jane [Wells?] or Nora [Haselden] or Brigit [Patmore] . . . it is interesting to speculate." I had asked for it & got it. But how can one be devoted to a cruel jester like that! Later he said, "You see I *can not* care for people with any constancy." It is queer. I felt I hated him at that moment and it gave me self-control. He only does it to annoy poor foolish vain baby!

Sun., June 3. Toothache.

Mon., June. 4.   ″

Tues., June 5. I had a *crise* in the night

Wed., June 6.   ″

---

[76] Redcar is a popular seaside resort in Yorkshire; Whitby, also in Yorkshire, is a picturesque harbor and fishing town. The Hunt family often summered in that area, where Alfred Hunt found subjects for his landscape painting.

[77] Nobble: a slang word meaning to tamper with a horse, as by drugging or laming it, in order to prevent it from winning a race. Ford is apparently carrying on a flirtation with the colonel's wife, and Hunt wants to squelch it. The colonel is Lt. Col. G. R. Powell, to whom Ford dedicated his volume of poems, *On Heaven* (1918).

Thurs., June 7.   I stopped a day longer—to remove the impression of Monday. I have to be self-controlled & look for no kindness from my "protector." I have to realize that no woe of mine or reaction from his stabs will move him to "let up." I have to defend myself by callousness. It is very queer. And no sort of life! I don't know him.

It's what is called a crank—or worse a degenerate. I get no more support from him than if he were my child

Fri., June 8.   F kissed me. I lent him £18 for his mess bill . . . He said he had liked having me there. Home—late—with difficulties

Sat., June 9.   I got in & settled. Am happier. *Il n'y a rien de donc comme le renoncement.* I shall have relapses of course. But now that I know the arms I long for *don't* press me very closely when I go to them, it is easier. It is like calling for a[n] anodyne that does not in fact soothe. But I do wish he would make our financial prospects more possible. It is up to me to imagine that I was just got up to the North so that I might meet the mess bill & I suppose I ought to think it. One's kindly vanity prevents. F is what Wells called him—a *mental* parasite. He will do all he can to get *mental* ease—he exerted just as much emotional fluid to get me as was required & has now turned off the tap. Well, he can't hurt *me* so much now—only my vanity & I must learn to let that go, or get others to satisfy it. Then age will come. So long as we don't lose each other but live on together inconvenienced but not solitary.

Sun., June 10.   He wrote he misses me & will more presently. He "wishes I wld believe he loves me" & save him the trouble of proving it! He "possesses me" he says, & nothing wld shake his conviction. I certainly do give him grounds for supposing it. But does he? He did! I don't know myself. I only know I find him an expensive luxury. I can't go near him but bang goes—much more than sixpence. To Mrs Arias in my new Recketts blue Wilson hat—a great an instantaneous success.

Mon., June 11.   Mrs Marley brought her Jeff to dine & Byles. Another world—the world of the Dover Patrol. Tall stories—true enough I daresay.

Tues., June 12.   To the Bank. F's affairs are hopeless. I ought to be out of them. He says so but takes no sort of step towards independence. The war is just one long laze for a man with a brain like F's. Dined Apperley.

Bought F 2 shirts & ordered him a pair of boots at Peals £4.10/. My new novel about Margt Sackville & F shall be called *Synthetic Love*[78]

Wed., June 13. To see C F Keary.[79] He is dying I *think*. Pernicious anemia

Thurs., June 14. Bellotti dinner. The Aldingtons[80] were there & Edgar Jepson. "You and F are absolutely suited to each other," he said. "You stimulate each other" .... "He is deeply attached to you."

Fri., June 15. Tea Mrs Dummett. I look well

Sat., June 16. F wires he comes on Sunday. It leaves me calm rather pleased but afraid. There is such a lot of self control needed ... & it is so boring. An awful thunderstorm. E Mayne here all aft.

Sun., June 17. Ford came in at 7. I had had tea at Mrs Chapmans— all serene

Mon., June 18. Lunched Masterman

Tues., June 19. A bad day. Shopping. F had a swimming head. Sat in the Park. F left at 5. Saw him off. The noise of the engine flustered him. He wasn't nice

Fri., June 22. Dined with A Watts[81] at the Automobile Club. When we came back to S L he treated me to a love scene—a declaration .... It ended You've no heart—no sex. And muddled, pleased, not in love with A Watts—would that I had been!—I let it go at that.

Sat., June 23. Saw A W. He is quite calm & reasonable. It does not offend me, as it would if I cared. And Capt Marno waited till Ezra and A W had gone, to say I "had wonderful eyes." Did I know?—He "did not want to pay me a compliment." He is only 27. London Regt. [VH: Did not materialize.]

[78] Lady Margaret Sackville (1881-1963) was a poet. The projected novel never materialized.

[79] Charles Francis Keary (1848-1917), the historical writer, novelist, and poet, actually died in October 1917.

[80] Richard Aldington (1892-1962), the poet and novelist, and his American-born wife, the poet Hilda Doolittle (1886-1961), were among the frequent guests at South Lodge.

[81] Arthur George Watts (1883-1935), artist and caricaturist, served in World War I and was a regular contributor to humorous magazines.

Sun., June 24.   Lunched Juliet's, tea at the new Mrs Austin Harrisons.[82] I enjoyed it. Austin roared like a mild little cosmopolitan-suburban lion . . .

Mon., June 25.   Richard Pryce[83] came to tea. We talked of novels— nought else . . .

Tues., June 26.   Tea at the McColls.[84] We had *white* bread—yet a baker in the neighborhood. McC has a famous, a beautiful Japanese screen.—I said where did you pick it up? & he replied apologetically, "Bond St."

Wed., June 27. Lunch George's

Thurs., June 28.   Bellotti dinner & on to Nora Haseldens. Fox Trot— bad for me

Fri., June 29.   I daresay I was in all day

Sat., June 30.   Dined at Café Royal with A Watts. Saw Epstein & Nevinson.[85] My gold hat & gold veil create sensation. I like it. A W tells me that it has flashed on him that F M H is a "pure inellectual." I like the phrase—useful! A W makes no love. I am glad. It *affermirs* me, though to know.

A telegram from the baby (intellectual) that his bicycle has been recovered.

Sun., July 1.   Nora came to see me. Dear little sad complacent common- place rival! Dined at Viva's—temperance dinner. So I indulged at home 11:30. It made me so friendly with the dead & loneliness—I walked in the dining room possessed with a sense of fellowship with those gone— I drank whisky & found myself saying (like Hamlet & his "fellow in the cellarage")[86]—"I'm only walking about on top a little bit longer & then"

---

82 Austin Harrison replaced Ford as editor of *The English Review* after Sir Alfred Mond bought it on Hunt's persuasion in 1909.

83 Richard Pryce (1864-1942) was a prolific novelist and playwright, born in France of English parents, known for his popular romantic and sentimental fiction.

84 Norman McColl was the editor of the *Athenaeum* at the time Margaret Hunt was a contributor.

85 The Café Royal on Regent Street was frequented by writers and artists, such as Wyndham Lewis (1884-1957) and the sculptor Jacob Epstein (1880-1959). Rich- ard (C. R. W.) Nevinson (1889-1946) was a well-known war painter, son of the famous journalist and war correspondent, H. W. Nevinson. Epstein and Nevinson were members of the Vorticist group that frequented South Lodge.

86 *Hamlet*, I, v, 151.

—After all, one is dead in the best company. Is it real, being dead? If I died now—I shld have no terrors. I am ill, but there is I believe no danger of a stroke—arteries all healthy. But I wonder? I don't love Ford —I am a queer side-bone of him.

Mon., July 2.   Metcalf's Hydro.

Tues., July 3.   Indigestion so bad I went to Richmond

Wed., July 4.   Ford quiescent—I too. And I am able to stay at home.

Thurs., July 5.   Not so peaceful. There is a row latent about Barclay's overdraft—over £10.

Fri., July 6.   To Chalfont St. Giles to stay with Mrs Gossage. Last time it was for the day only, & 3 years ago. And she asked after "Madam Bridget?" Not knowing—Now there has been a Miss Ross between! Mrs G has "no guts" mentally. Physically, has had an operation.

Sat., July 7.   I don't think *much* of Ford. We heard the great reverberation of guns on Harewood Downs. We thought it was practise at Chorley Wood.[87] Later reports came in. One couldn't phone to London or send a wire. General P. O. burning. Boats—& so on! Later on 2 tired bleached women workers came down & hardly spoke of the raid till tea was in them.

Sun., July 8.   Commander Sparrow[88] came. He had a part view from *a bas*!

Mon., July 9.   Home. I brought C[ommander] S[parrow]'s clubs & bag & my own two with infinite difficulty, being helped at every stage by wounded soldiers.

Tues., July 10.   Byles came. Norman Smith[89] in Cannon St dictated

[87] Harewood Downs are in Yorkshire, Chorley Woods in Lancashire. That morning, London suffered a massive German air raid in which 37 were killed and 141 injured. About twenty German planes took part in the raid.

[88] Colonel Richard Sparrow (1871-1953), C.M.G., D.S.O., was commanding officer of the 7th Dragoon Guards. He served four years in France during World War I and retired in 1920. In her story "The Cigarette Case of the Commander" (1925), Hunt recreates the image of the ignored woman resentfully carrying the commander's clubs home.

[89] Norman Kemp Smith (1872-1958) was professor of psychology at Princeton University, but spent 1916 to 1918 doing war work in London. Afterwards he became professor of logic and metaphysics at Edinburgh. He was known for his translations and commentaries on Descartes, Hume, and Kant.

some letters & then took me out to Little Queen St where a house was wrecked & ten people killed. It looked very like a photograph. Then a shell hole filled in, very like a scab of a sore on the plain straight street. Byles dined

Wed., July 11. To see *Les Avariés* in its English.[90] Took Valerie Marley. I went & saw Mary Gray (Mrs Fagan) in her room

Thurs., July 12. F writes—quite nicely. I am nearly getting over my unpleasant *secousse* when I open his letters lest they contain a new strafe. He says he is tired & that the work is too much for him. Dined Bellotti. Miss Barry[91] is rather interesting. Little boys in the street after the raid were selling small pieces of German black bread fallen out of the aeroplanes. I feel better. Miss D's [B?] remarks help me to think wisely for myself. F she says is an elemental . . . a male Undine,[92] compact mostly of water . . . .

Fri., July 13. Tea Mrs Head's. I heard Ford did threaten in a club to prosecute Dr Head for abusing him & divulging professional secrets.[93] It makes my path easier. He is not responsible

Sat., July 14. Miss Barry & Mrs Farrant to tea. Both workers. How different their outlook

Sun., July 15. To Jepsons, talk of poison-bombs launched by aerial torpedoes with a radius of 300 yards

[90] Eugene Brieux's *Les Avariés* played in London at the St. Martin's Theatre in an English translation, under the title *Damaged Goods*. Its London run was so successful that in April of 1917 a second edition of John Pollock's translation of the play, with George Bernard Shaw's Preface, was published.

[91] Iris Barry (b. 1895) was a young poet from Birmingham, recently discovered by Ezra Pound. Pound encouraged her to leave Birmingham for London, which she did in 1917, joining as this entry indicates his dinner group at Bellotti's. In October 1931, she recalled "The Ezra Pound Period" for *The Bookman*, remembering Violet Hunt, "chattering with sublime disregard for practically everything, distraught golden hair, obviously a beauty of the Edwardian era . . . disconcerting for the way she pounced . . . at once good natured and sharp-tongued."

[92] Undine is a female water spirit who acquires a human soul by marriage, but she is eventually reclaimed by her natural element. In Fouqué's fairy romance (1811), Undine is roguish and bewitching before her marriage; Ford is here being accused of lacking a soul, of being so amorphous that he is impossible to pin down.

[93] Dr. Head was Ford's physician. Hunt recognized that in accusing his doctor of divulging professional secrets, Ford was following the same pattern he had in accusing her of blackening his name.

Mon., July 16.   Dined Defries. F writes to say he fancies he is being "ill wished." I have heard that before—*histoire de Brigitte.*

Tues., July 17.   Dined Mrs Dummetts Wallas[94] & Colonel Fletcher. Dull, good dinner. *C'est déjà quelque chose.* F is gone. "Not in town. People turn me against him." Not people but oh, my God, how turned!

Thurs., July 19.   Bellotti dinner. Mrs Farrant & Mrs Pennell. A Watts walked in mufti or rather navy evening dress—he did not try to get to me. Mrs M at my elbow said significantly "I should never forgive him"

Fri., July 20.   The mystery solved. A Watts had rung me up & tried to get me to dine. So he dined alone first & then came in & went out with Ezra to get something. Then—he returned. I went with Mrs P[ennell]. Tonight at the Carmen Brooks they danced & I did not. I felt as if A W & I were married & had got to *that* stage of indifference & kind feeling. He is very young & danced well. A girl called Stella Bowen[95] came in with Ezra & I was, I suppose a little jealous of her. Yet why I could have him. Why I would if I liked him physically as well as F—whom I hate rather. I would not go on to Stella B's—in her studio—more dancing that I can't share. I let them all get into a cab & walked home & took a whisky & soda. Why? I felt—failure, annoyance—I wanted to ring him up at Morley's Hotel. I will tomorrow. Foolish if I wanted to pique him. But I don't. I rather miss him. That's all. And it makes me feel less kind to F.

Sat., July 21.   I rang A W up this morning & wished I had not. He as good as owned that he was trying to forget me. To "Where are my Children?"[96] with Mrs Leopold Hirsch.[97] I am depressed. I can't somehow write to Ford. *Mon métier a disparu.*

---

[94] Graham Wallas (1858-1932) lectured on political science at the London School of Economics and was an early member of the Fabian Society. As usual, Hunt is bored by politics in the abstract.

[95] This date marks the first appearance of Stella Bowen, the young (twenty-four at this time) Australian painter come to study at the Westminster School of Art. Apparently, Stella is dancing with Watts, and Hunt, who does not at this point in her life participate in dancing, reacts instinctively, jealously. Ironically, Hunt will soon have real reason to be jealous, as Stella supplants her in Ford's life.

[96] "Where Are My Children" was sponsored by the National Council of Public Morals and was performed at Philharmonic Hall.

[97] Mrs. Leopold Hirsch sat for Sargent. When Hunt was selling copies of the Vorticist periodical *Blast* at a party at South Lodge, "She bought one, but returned her copy next day with a nice letter pointing out that I might perhaps doubly benefit

Sun., July 22. Reeve Wallace, Mrs Adam Sedgwick[98] and Miss Tennyson Jesse[99] lunched. It is so funny entertaining without Ford & yet I can't imagine entertaining *with* him now. And I did not go out

Mon., July 23. In. Busy. F's *Women & Men*[100] has come back from Mrs Fallas. To Ethel Mayne's. I am not F's mistress. I can't be his friend. I *won't* be his wife.

Thurs., July 26. Ford's sports. He wanted me to go to R[edcar] for them. I could not.

Fri., July 27. Ethel Redley & Mrs Pennell. Dined Capt M[arno] in the evening. He is a Fairfax on the mother's side, a Spaniard on father's: 27. "This is my bridal night!" he said. I am in a fair way to be a *Ninon de l'Enclos.*[101] One could be worse, for at any rate she was a philosopher. But I *une amoureuse*, which she was not! It is strange.

Sat., July 28. To Miss Bowens studio. Margt Postgate[102] sister of a conscientious objector there. I am being slowly changed. F will not know me again. He will be puzzled—so long as I do not revert. There has been

---

the author by reselling it to someone who hadn't daughters. She really couldn't have it lying about for there was a poem in the volume by Ezra Pound which youth must on no account pick up and read" (*I Have This to Say*, p. 215).

[98] Mrs. Adam Sedgwick (née Laura Robinson of Armagh) was the widow of Adam Sedgwick, who was professor of zoology at the Imperial College of Science and Technology at South Kensington.

[99] F[riniwyd] Tennyson Jesse (1899-1958), the great-niece of Alfred Tennyson, took up journalism during World War I. In 1918 she married H. M. Harwood the dramatist and collaborated with him in a number of plays. She was best known as a novelist and editor of several volumes of the *Notable British Trials* series.

[100] *Women and Men* (1923) is Ford's collection of essays, originally published separately in *The Little Review*. Ford was at work on this project as early as 1911; he had begun it on the theory that it would sell widely among the suffragists.

[101] Ninon (Anne) de L'Enclos (1616-1706) had a long amorous career in seventeenth-century France. Her lovers included many noblemen, among them the Duc de Larochefoucauld. She was as celebrated for her manners as for her beauty, so much so that respectable women sent their children to her for schooling in courtesy.

[102] Margaret Postgate (b. 1893) was an active member of the Fabian Society, employed by the Fabian Research Department from 1917 to 1926. She later became Honorary Secretary of the society. Her husband G. D. H. Cole, whom she married in 1918, was also an active Fabian and a professor of social and political theory at Oxford. She and her husband wrote a number of social and political works, as well as detective novels.

a row broken heads "The Daily Express" people silencing a Pacifist meeting[103]

Sun., July 29. Rebecca West lunched. She is so poetically scandalous. Jane Anderson that she went "munitioning" with, under the auspices of the Govt escorted by Lloyd G[eorge]'s[104] drunken secretary (*not* Dike) is a German spy, now gone to Northcliffe in America *pour surcroît* (tracked down by Boyle O'Reilly, my enemy.) Then Stella Bowen & Phillis Reid[105] came in. Dined at W L Georges. Capt Marno escorted me back. Quite mad.

Mon., July 30. To Deways for Ford. Bought a dress . . . Byles dined

Tues., July 31. Packed nearly all day & some devastating work. Rebecca came in for her hat she had left in Sunday's storm & talked of her Australian, whom, now he has died she finds she loved. She is as absorbed in H G's [Wells] noncontentment of her[106] as I *was* in F's . . . . of me. She runs on & sighs & groans & has got H G tight because of it

Wed., Aug. 1. 8 to 6 travelling to Ford—a stranger on Redcar platform. He is jovial, casual, strangely dull, & had a cold. *Donc pas de tendresse* . . . And I could not sleep, & yet I don't love him.

Sat., Aug. 4. The night he permits himself to be passionate. He was not: only brutal & coarse.

Sun., Aug. 5. A tea picnic. Col Powell drove me.

Mon., Aug. 6. We argued a *little* over my bedside

Tues., Aug. 7. Same

---

[103] The pacifist meeting Hunt refers to was a conference to form a Workers' and Soldiers' Council in London, broken up by the attack of an angry crowd. Part of the church the pacifists were meeting in was wrecked and some delegates injured.

[104] David Lloyd George (1863-1945) held to a pacifist position before the war, but changed when Germany threatened the invasion of Belgium. In 1915 he was appointed minister of munitions, in 1916 war secretary, and he served as coalition prime minister from 1916 to 1922.

[105] Phyllis Reid shared a flat with Stella Bowen.

[106] The summer of 1917 was a difficult one for Wells and West. She was unnerved by her isolation at Leigh-on-Sea, by the frequent bombing raids, and by Wells's behavior towards her. In September he wrote chastizing West for her unhappiness: "All the past four years which might have been a love-adventure in our memories, your peculiar genius has made into an utterly disagreeable story—which has become the basis for an entire hopelessness about anything yet to come" (Ray, p. 80).

Wed., Aug. 8.   ″

Thurs., Aug. 9.   I am bored to death. I made up my mind to get it in first so I said "Well, I'm tired & I'm going to my own bed!" He kissed me & said "All right darling!" Then later when I was in bed, I repented & *asked* him to sleep with me. Mrs P[owell] had advised it. He began "Well-ell!"—And it was all over. We did not quarrel or I cry, but it seemed *again* (it has happened twice before) as if the end of the world had come . . . He said "I didn't want you for *that*—just for quiet companionship." And I said "That was no good to me!" No quarrel. I said "Kiss me & go!" I felt that there wasn't anything to say. There never will be again. I ought to go—or tell him to go & live in camp as before I came. But of course that—the only way to bring him to his bearings—is impossible, as it would make talk. I ought not to have come without a *laisser passer*. I have raged all day—alone. I must *not* let him know.

Sat., Aug. 11.   To the Aerodrome Display & left at 5 with F. Ford said "I made up my mind to give up Sat. to you & I will." Then I asked him to deposit me & go back.

Sun., Aug. 12.   F golfed with Moxey in the morning & brought him home to lunch. Then he went a bicycle picnic to Lockwood Beck with the Powells & others. Returned at 9, drenched & to bed.

Mon., Aug. 13.   He was unkind. We did not speak all day much.

All day silent. At night I said I could not go on like this: & that I wld not come again or see him again unless he felt "keener" about me. He is like a slug, or the cuttlefish that throws out venom to annoy & obscure the issue. Admit a necessity for parting! Not he! He turns sleepy comatose & gets out of the discussion by saying that *I* am not serious.

Tues. morning, Aug. 14.   He came into my room. Tea: I said "Aren't you going to kiss me?" He said "It depends on what terms we are on." I said "On the only terms that are possible for us—badly as we may interpret them." I didn't say those words exactly but that is the sense. I meant that we must be ineffectual lovers but lovers—or else part. As a matter of terms, I mean. He understood. He lay down. He said I killed all movement towards me by such speeches as "I may as well sleep badly with you because you snore & take up the room as sleep badly because we are estranged." I said "You admire my books for their grimness: there it is!" F wants to run with the hare & hunt with the hound. He wants me the romantic sweetheart & the German hausfrau rolled in one. In short a quiet companion & a loving *pâmée* mistress . . . . And as far as I can see it is the Web of Maia[107] for me. Conflicting emotions & wills. The army as an *échappatoire* for him.

Tues., Aug. 21.   I haven't kept the wretched thing [the diary.] I never shall. F & I had a *fearful* row three night ago, Saturday of course, the one night he can "afford to be passionate" on—for no parade on Sunday. He *denied* absolutely having written to Miss Ross that letter I hold. That settled it all. I hit him & then took him to bed. He is not sane. Then on Sunday we played cricket—I too! No more rows—or relatives. Monday another little row—*sans suites.* We shall settle down as soon as I have *quite* given up trying to remake him in my own image. I shall be indurated presently. The rows will go or be like the big drops at the end of a shower. He is absolutely irresponsible & *a-moral.* It is absurd to break a butterfly—a tolerably substantial one—on the wheel & I shall learn not to. But meantime if I keep the dreary peace until I go, & realize that F is an elemental spirit: absolutely incapable of emotion at first hand. What *I* am doing in this *galère*! It is awful to look into his cold blue eyes & see no spark of warmth there. But to keep alive the regret for old unhappy far off things the days I lent him all my emotion & wondered why he did not speak in supreme moments. Why should he? It is only a physical exercise with him. I went to Durham to see Rosamond[108] & her children. I took [in] W[illiam] G[reenwell][109] on my way. It was an adventure. He is 97. I saw Rushworth & he took me. The old man did not know me. I kissed him. Then the old Wesley—staying with him (77) raked up his card game & wailed. I get an overpowering impression of caducity. Then Rushworth said, "Your goddaughter Sir!" And the old

---

[107] Maia, loveliest of the Pleiades, was the mother of Hermes by Zeus. Her name means simply "mother" or "nurse." Hunt sees herself caught in the Web of Maia by Ford's desire that she be both lovely pleiad and "German hausfrau" who will mother and nurse him.

[108] Rosamond is the daughter of Violet's sister Silvia, and a favorite niece for whom she nurtured a maternal affection. Hunt delighted in chaperoning the young north-country girl, whom she called "The Beauty," around London, but Silvia disapproved of Violet as a companion for her daughter. As the scandal of the Ford-Hunt affair grew, Silvia withdrew her daughter from the society of her aunt. Violet was distraught at the separation, although Rosamond had developed a flirtatious relationship with Ford, which both he and Violet were aware of.

[109] Hunt was the god-daughter of Canon William Greenwell, a well-known archaeologist. The year before this episode, Greenwell, grown "tetchy" in his old age and unhappy about Violet's personal life, had cut her out of his will, leaving his money to his nurse and favorite verger, probably the Freeman who is mentioned in this episode.

man's face changed set in a vindictive mouth grip, & he flopped round in his chair & said "Damn!" He would not speak to me. I stood, with my back to a roaring fire while old Wesley cowered in the background, and argued with him gently. He repeated "I wish to have nothing to do with you!" and "You are not his wife." Then I went down to Anne & ate my lunch I had brought in her sitting room, while W G & Wesley & Freeman the verger had theirs in the dining room. I had to pass them all to go out & did it I am thankful to say with my head high. That is the end of my mother's romance. That is how she & he broke—the reason why he was not my father!

Ford was orderly for the day & did not come in till 11:30, after I was in bed having got back from Middlesboro at 9. The strike[110] seems not to be coming off: but they are still mobilized.

Wed., Aug. 22.   A "standby," all mobilized.

Thurs., Aug. 23.   The Powells could not leave

Fri., Aug. 24.   They left. The army regt. is demobilized. We saw the P's off. F is I am sure, *amouraché* of Mrs Powell, a terrible, plain, flirt— the worst[111]

Sat., Aug. 25.   We walked to Kirkleatham, dreary. A row at night. F has gone sick. His face is all scratched—by me.

Sun., Aug. 26.   The awfullest day ... mostly together, but dreary. F declares himself "impotent"—That is the latest.

Mon., Aug. 27.   I am going on Wed., to give up here. F wants to live with me, for "quiet companionship" only. I can't. It irritates me too much for him to talk of it

Tues., Aug. 28.   Lunch & tea at the Aerodrome

Wed., Aug. 29.   Instead of going sensibly home I decided to go to the Coatham, a room alone. Partly for convenience—I had run my packing rather fine—& to show Ford I could stand living away from him—And this is how it would be if he lived apart from me in London. He would

---

110 The strike referred to is a national railway strike in which the men were pressing for an eight-hour day. By August 23, the *Times* reported that the danger of strike had been averted.

111 Hunt was jealous of the colonel's wife because she had helped Ford select the poems for *On Heaven*. Ford then compounded the insult by belittling in his preface the volume's title poem, which he had dedicated to Hunt.

be so savage at my not caring to *live* with him that he would not be nice to me. It is horrid & I could not sleep for worry. But ever since he told me that I "made no effort to be attractive to him"—& that I ought "to be more elusive" I am so awkward with him that *no* position is tenable. I believe we ought to part. I shall perhaps be strong enough to write him to that effect when I am away.

Thurs., Aug. 30.   It is very dull.

Fri., Aug. 31.   A row, because I say I want to go home on Sat! He "resents it—as an insult to him." He is mad. I *must* try not to care. I *have* to get it into my head that he is oblique . . . . I agreed late at night to stay till Monday.

Sat., Sept. 1.   Spent a rainy morning in undoing all my arrangements for home. A row with F that night

Sun., Sept. 2.   I ought not to have stayed. We entertained largely all day. The Hoggans (Major, Second in Command) to dinner. Billiards. Then F wanted to sleep with me in the literal sense "cushy & agreeable" —I tried to arouse him: In vain. He said "Do I worry you" & I said "Well, rather." The idea is that he is distressed at his impotence, which I don't believe in—how should I?—& I remind him. A fearful row—we still talk of parting, which is absurd as we neither of us mean to. He said "The only way to end this quarrel is for you to go quietly to your own bed & say no more about it in the morning." Just what I can't. And he is right. I know why he is unhappy & *absorbed*. He owes £10 on a bet made in Nov 1916 to say the war would be over in June 1917 when he stood to win £50. It is with Grismond Phillips who has reminded him. He doesn't tell me so I can't know. We parted friends but I feel that we can't ever be together again on these terms & it is so serious that I can't tell him. I tried to get out on an unreal patching. He came as far as Middlesborough with me for which jaunt of his I paid 7/6. He had no money on him. Poor poor dear and I held him for a moment—he was kinder than he has been for 5 weeks—in the train & *knew* it meant nothing but both our good will to part picturesquely. An awful journey no cab from Kings X—underground clogged

Tues., Sept. 4.   Byles came. The raid. Bad! Up all night.

Wed., Sept. 5.   The storms. I sent F £10 cheque to send Phillips. He will be enraged. He has not written anyway. Dined with Mrs Pennell.

Thurs., Sept. 6. No letter from F. I felt very miserable in spite of my resolved indifference. Ethel Mayne says I am *exigeante*, but that now there is only one course open to me, to deny my—physical—society to F, without discussion or possibility of change. At Bellottis asked Stella Bowen & Phillis Reid to come to Selsey while F there. He asked for "something young"

Fri., Sept. 7. F wrote—a very poor letter but I daresay all I deserve. Ethel Mayne says I am an *exigeante* devil. Odd—F detests her & yet she always takes his side. The truth is I can't love him enough to *like* him— his ways with me.

Sat., Sept. 8. F wrote. And I wrote. That letter from Grismond Phillips! Now confirmation. Porterfield on leave says all the Regt is talking of it & F's non payment. I wrote F to that effect enclosing a cheque to G P saying I wld make it good. A showerbath string pulled.

Sun., Sept. 9. To Mrs Arias. Two actresses, Gilbert Frankau,[112] the W L Georges made a harmonious string. G F said I was the writer of the best short story in the English language *The Tiger Skin*.[113] Dined Mrs Pitt Lewis.

Mon., Sept. 10. Ford denies ever betting £10 & never will. Says G[rismond] P[hillips] may say what he likes about him in Cardiff & will . . . I ought to have known F wouldn't admit. But I guess he'll pay & the cheque will be debited to *my* account, as I said. This is the limit! Yet I suppose there is no limit—? I am so sad. Dined with Stella Bowen & Phillis Reid (great beauty).

Tues., Sept. 11. Mrs Pennell & E Mayne to tea. A violent anti-pacifist discussion. Byles dined

Wed., Sept. 12. The young Nevinsons Mrs Pennell & Apperley dined. Very gay. N very ill & very pessimistic. A draw.

Thurs., Sept. 13. F says he has *paid* the £10 to Phillips—and so the matter ended.

---

[112] Gilbert Frankau (1884-1952), poet, novelist, and short-story writer, served in France and Italy during World War I and was invalided from the service with shell-shock in 1918. *The Guns* (1916) was his volume of war poems.

[113] *The Tiger Skin*, a long story about sex, eugenics, and child abuse, was published separately in book form in 1924 and included in Hunt's collection, *More Tales of the Uneasy*, 1925.

Fri., Sept. 14.   Opposite Mudie's[114] I met Flint—puis Jean de Bochère[115] then Holmes on leave. Funny how they start geniuses. J de B translated by Flint: pref. by May Sinclair.[116] Saw Ethel Mayne. She says I *must* just let things go & cease to try to alter them.

Sat., Sept. 15.   Keary. He says "our" only chance is a firm friendship. Tea with Cecilly Colls. She is coming to Selsey

Sun., Sept. 16.   Tea at Mrs Allens, aunt of Mrs "Ikey" Somerset. She launched out into abuse of Rossie, my husband's flirtation. Everyone knows. Rossie *accaparied* him—weak as all men are. She was Braine's mistress. Poor old futile Ford. He thinks he has got an ingénue, & its a garrison hack. Now he has nobody. He hates me.

Tues., Sept. 18. Dined Registers. They are so kind & so suburban, it is refreshing. I feel as if Ford was a malignant elf—sure to annoy but I do hope nothing will happen to him! I suppose the reason we can't now get on is that I persist in regarding myself as a romantic figure, & no one is to be romantic but F M H. Paul Register—70-odd is wonderful. Rose Register has been ill—she went to sleep. He was at a city dinner & had to wear court dress—knee breeches, silk stockings etc. He told someone that it was an odd sensation the feel of silk stockings on his own legs! A flirt. Now to my loveless bed!

Thurs., Sept. 20.   Ethel Redley to tea. Dined Bellotti with Miss Colls

Fri., Sept. 21.   Raid. Bad

Sat., Sept. 22.   To Richmond Bath. It tired me. F writes stupidly

Sun., Sept. 23.   Dined at Chinese Restaurant with Mrs Pennell

Mon., Sept. 24.   More raid

[114] Mudie's Select Library, the circulating library, was located on New Oxford Street, with a branch on Brompton Road.

[115] F[rank] S[tewart] Flint (1885-1960), a member of the Imagist movement, published lyric poetry and produced many translations. He was an occasional guest at South Lodge. In 1917 he translated a collection of poems, *The Closed Door*, by the French poet Jean de Bosschere.

[116] May Sinclair (1865-1946) was, along with Ethel Mayne, Hunt's warmest friend and strongest supporter. She shared Hunt's passions for suffrage, psychology, novel writing, and cats. Of Hunt's affair with Ford, although she advised Violet to stay out of the country until the furor calmed, she maintained that she did not at all care whether their marriage was legal in England, or even whether it had taken place. She also wrote in *The English Review* (February 1922) a generous appreciation of Hunt as an accomplished novelist.

Tues., Sept. 25.   Richmond. Took Stella Bowen to Parisian Restaurant

Wed., Sept. 26.   Ford asks me to York for 3 days. *Can't!*

Thurs., Sept. 27.   To Jepsons & to see a new doctor. *Shuter.* He says I am neurasthenic.

Fri., Sept. 28.   Birthday—only Child with her yearly purse (I lose em) to wish me M[any] H[appy] R[eturns of the] D[ay]. But one is too old. Mrs Marley had a dinner for me, and a view of air raid: which did *not* come off.[117] We sat in the kitchen in the roof with the windows wide open, an uncomfortable kitchen table, & looked out. A bicycle & man ringing a bell besought us to "take cover." The streets were empty. Then we heard guns dully. Then no more. I went home at 11—I heard the "all clear!" was given at 10:30. They did not get nearer than Pitsea Island. The traffic on underground stopped for 2 hours. The Southend train 2 hrs late passed me as I spoke—They would not get to S tonight.

Sat., Sept. 29.   F writes apprehensively about my terrors. Raids. There was a very bad one tonight. I was at Mrs. Pitt Lewis. Behind closed shutters. Mary I & she sewing for dear life round the dining room table. After, I saw the whole street, in the blanching moonlight, engaged in seeking for shrapnel. White figures like mushrooms under the full blaze —Child at home, Harriet said, nearly fainted.

Sun., Sept. 30.   Worse. A bomb (mis)exploded in C[ampden] H[ill] Road. Campden House Court. I joined the crowd, hunted for shrapnel. The Boothes were there. Some loud women took exception to me, swore at the German B——ys, and said there were "Germans in that crowd." Almost followed me home . . . The noise was not so bad as last night. Some shrapnel must have hit the lead roof. It is beautiful moonlight. Child goes tomorrow to Selsey I not till Thursday. Funny to have a German—nor husband nor lover—but reputedly both . . .

Mon., Oct. 1.   Saw Child off. It is all very rough, & continental *laissez aller*, not *laisser faire*. The passengers have to close the doors themselves sort themselves . . . No porters, all fighting. Child & I carried in a large dress box between us—in despair of haughty, unique porter who at last relented & carried the rest. I saw a woman who had secured a barrow wheel her own luggage through the gates & on to the platform. I stayed

---

117 On September 29 the *Times* reported an air raid that failed to reach metropolitan London. Planes, however, did attack the east and southeast coast, dropping bombs in Suffolk, Essex, and Kent.

in after, to tea, but no one came—not Mrs Osborne of Cardiff! Mrs Braine has told her not to, perhaps? The raid tonight, if it is over 10 to 11, was milder much. Wrote to Arthur Watts—he wrote a week ago. I want all the love I can get. And although he has the face of a gnome, he *is* something. Ford he calls a "pure intellectual." The pure I[ntellectual] can descend to some very earthy phenomena.

Tues., Oct. 2. I did what I wanted. Left Harriet here to go to *her* flat for the night & where she feels safer, and saw Compton Mackenzie,[118] & dined with Mrs Stafford (Mrs Marleys mother) & Car. There was no night raid. The clouds came over the moon. I expect the enemy realised the barometric change & had their meal of hate in the middle of the day. Saw Mrs Ryan [VH: American journalist]—there will be paragraph in the *Weekly Despatch*—about my wearing Ford's tin helmet.[119] I did. It *was* nice, no raid.

Wed., Oct. 3. To see Ford's mother & sister & Ethel Mayne. Then dined Goodie's. Nell to lunch. Wrote to F. He wants to end letters Goodbye, dear—so much easier! & I said he may. I don't care.

Thurs., Oct. 4. Just as I was starting for Selsey to meet Ethel Redley at Victoria, a wire from F to say he has asked for leave tonight! Am I going to Selsey. No time to reply, did not want to. Selsey as usual. I shook hands with Allen[120] on the platform. I am afraid a sort of defiance of F.

---

[118] Compton Mackenzie (1883-1972), British novelist, poet, and playwright, became director of the Aegean Intelligence Service in Syria in 1917. In his memoirs he recalls attending parties at South Lodge, at one of which he was first introduced to Rebecca West.

[119] Grace Lovat Fraser recounts the tin hat episode: "I remember with amusement one such raid party which was an invitation affair. To it came Violet Hunt and Ford Madox Ford, who was on leave. Violet, with inspired sartorial genius, arrived wearing Ford's 'tin hat' firmly anchored to her head by a broad pink satin ribbon tied in a bow under her chin. Her entrance was hilariously greeted and she took this very well; but I have never been quite sure whether she wore the helmet as a joke or as a serious attempt at protection" (*In the Days of My Youth* [London: Cassell, 1970], pp. 239-40).

[120] Edward Heron-Allen (1861-1943), an old friend of Hunt and her family, lived at Selsey Bill, Sussex. A marine biologist and zoologist, Heron-Allen was from 1916-18 the President of the Royal Microscopical Society. He was also a writer, bibliophile, and translator, with books on violin-making, historical and pre-historical Selsey, and Fitzgerald's *Omar Khayyám*. Violently anti-German (he was attached to the Staff Intelligence Dept. War Office in 1918), he was particularly upset at Violet's association with Ford. For his part, Ford satirically depicted Allen in a November 1914 story, "The Scaremonger," which appeared in the *Bystander*.

79

Fri., Oct. 5 to Fri., Oct. 12.   Water pipes wrong—a bill—we can't use the kitchen at all. Three men in all day. Writing & wiring to F all the time I had hemorrhage,[121] and he seems to think I want him. He said "get Barford to write & say you are dying: then they will give me leave." I did not. But I wired "come 20th not 22. Most important." Fatal! I meant Stella Bowen would be going on Wed. [VH: She was with me] Allen wrote nastily about the pipes addressing me as Mrs V. Hunt Hueffer. It was perhaps responsible for my 3rd hemorrhage. A[llen] thinks I made up, in order to induce him to stand water repair bill.

Sat., Oct. 13.   Tea at André's.[122] Spoke to Nora

Mon., Oct. 22.   F turned up. Very angry at my telegram. Said he had cancelled weeks leave in order to come to me for 48 hrs. All was lost when Stella B going out of the room he threw his arms round me & kissed me. I *could* not respond. He turned sour. At night, after she had gone, he said coldly "Well, I'm going to bed"—(I had given him the big double bed & stayed in my own small bedroom). Then I made my first mistake. I exclaimed "And is this all—you have come all this way for— after all this time!"

No more amenity. Yet he makes me go to his bed & lie in his arms for a time. I hate it. He says he is *not* impotent, but he can't have *me*— "I could have you through another woman." That is simply to say he is tired of me. I realised it & had the sense not to say anything. I just went. He kissed me. I said "Don't be rough because of my nose bleeding again" & he said with pride "I *am* rough!"

Tues., Oct. 23.   He explained at greater length his impotency *a mon égard*. He says "I suppose I want adventure." "If I could have another woman I might desire *you*. I was nice to you in the Brigit time." It seemed perverted, but F is so queer. I took it calm.

Wed., Oct. 24.   He got an extension, but will spend 24 hrs in London. S Bowen will stop till Thursday & go with him. On Wed the real bloody row was—it resulted from a speech of mine. He said before we went to bed that he couldn't love or think of making love till he was no longer worried to death about money. He is overdrawn. Then when he wants

---

121 Hunt's hemorrhages were caused by syphilis.

122 Marc-André Raffalovitch (1865-1934) belonged to a wealthy family of Russian Jewish bankers in Paris. He was a member of Wilde's circle, a friend of Beardsley's, a frequent host of parties, and an occasional confidant of Hunt's. He is also known for his pioneering study of male homosexuality, *Uranisme et Unisexualité*.

money he is civil to me kisses me, because I "show comprehension!" I said I would again give a temporary guarantee. He kicked at "temporary." Still we went to bed together & lay in still, chill silence as usual. Then I said bitterly that I had thought he had been different downstairs (at the moment I had promised to—give money). He raged said it was filthy of me to taunt him, that he had asked me as a sort of test & that when one lent one didn't insult too—It was true, & I was ashamed, but when he told me not to "whine in a voice like a creaking door," I lost all control & pinched & buffeted him. He lies like a jelly fish instead of taking me by the wrists & stopping me. It is contemptible. And *then* he said "If you'll stop this disgusting exhibition & let me speak I'll tell you what I'll do. If I go away & have a quiet time for a couple of months I'll get leave at Xmas & then by that time I'll be able to make love to you." That was the limit. I went to my own bed. I hardly spoke next morning. They left. At that moment poor old C [F] Keary died of heart failure. He had provoked it, he told me

Thurs., Oct. 25.   I wrote to F saying how deadly ashamed I was & how I could not wish a repetition, but I did not love him enough to preserve my self control when he tormented me.

Sat., Oct. 27.   We left, Child & I. Then

Sun., Oct. 28.   I found a letter from F. He said "our silly troubles, which he wished we had not had" had not in the least "affected his permanent feeling for me."

Mon., Oct. 29.   To Dolleymores re the final distribution of Mother's things

Tues., Oct. 30.   Lunched Byles. I made him read my letter that Ford will call an ultimatum. I said, I'll put the copy in line. It is the end of the world—that world at least but I shall feel better, not in a false position, not sailing under the false flag. F's friend. Nothing is changed. I have only legalised our separation as it were

Wed., Oct. 31.   Raid, awakened by whistles "Take cover!" at midnight. At ½ past 12 it began. I went down to the kitchen with Cheeky [VH: cat] & sat there with Child for 2 hrs. We made ourselves some Horlick. Then after a long pause, I went up to bed & was *wakened* again by the bugles. All clear!

Thurs., Nov. 1. We are only "allowed"—we don't really have freedom to exist. The grave yawns for us all the time.

Genius say good things & don't *know* they're good. I am drunk. Ford never answers. He is *not my* romantic objective!

Sat., Nov. 3. Watts is married to Valentine Sanzi

Sun., Nov. 4. W L George's. Nevinson says that Govt. will have to repudiate bonds! A fearfully anti-social statement

Mon., Nov. 5. Dined Stella Bowen & Phillis Reid. My nose is so bad. F wrote saying "I will, then, not reply to your letter. Indeed I don't see what I could reply" .... Laufer was in asking me if I would care to take the Powells house at Redcar.

Tues., Nov. 6. The lump of mucous in my nose came away: I feel like a woman who has had a baby. To tea with old Stone in Curzon St— how old-fashioned! A Watts & Ethel Mayne in the evening. Watts says "reading 'The House of Many Mirrors'[123] is like being in a court house without a luncheon hour"

Wed., Nov. 7. Dr. Shuter. Electric exam: proves that I have no septum. To a certain extent I am like old Edward Fairfield with half his nose eaten away. I will not tell Ford. It seems as if the author of all my *maux* was O.C.[124]

Thurs., Nov. 8. Arthur Watts dined us all—the Bowen & Reid & May Sinclair at Bellotti's. He is improved. They all went & danced. I came home with Iris Barry—tired.

F writes & asks me to come to York.

Fri., Nov. 9. Lunched with Michael Heseltine at Villa-Villa.[125] Things —the war, Italy & Russia are so bad that we couldn't speak of them. F wires—etc & is coldly insistent on my presence. He would *like* me to come to York ....

Sat., Nov. 10. The Scott James[126]—he on leave from the *dangerous* gunner post dined. And Michael Heseltine.

[123] Hunt's novel, *The House of Many Mirrors*, was published in 1915.

[124] The OC Hunt refers to was her previous lover, Oswald Crawford, former British attaché at Oporto and editor of the journal *Black & White*.

[125] Villa-Villa, a restaurant in Soho, was located in a house once occupied by Edmund Burke.

[126] R[olfe] A[rnold] Scott-James (1878-1959) served as literary editor of the *Daily News* from 1906 to 1912 and leader writer for the *Daily Chronicle* from 1919 to 1930. He later became an editor of *The Spectator* and a literary critic.

Sun., Nov. 11. Lunched Mrs Dummett & C Graham.[127] They said Rebecca's style was shocking. Tea at Miss Miévilles—to Ethel Maynes—her Pacifist talk is awful. She says I am hard on Ford who is trying to get things "cooshy" again

Tues., Nov. 13. Byles dined. To Mrs Fletcher. Byles says the line of least resistance is the only one for me. But Ford dominates me to such an extent I *can't* keep up an attitude. I spend my thoughts on thinking what I shall say when he offers to come & see me. Then I bring myself up with a jerk for perhaps Fate won't let me have the chance. It's *like* Fate!

Wed., Nov. 14. If he asks to come I shall say Come if you care to stay with me under the new régime. But no. I *can't* force myself to swallow the long long affront his behavior to me is. Can I? And if I do, *qu'est-ce que je gagne*. Perhaps all—that is there to gain? The line of least resistance is wounding to one's pride . . . and perhaps if persisted in, saving of one's pride. I *can* give Ford what he wants, tho' he can't give me what I want.

Thurs., Nov. 15. Lunched with "Tessie"—at the Salonika.

Fri., Nov. 16. Goode's. Pacifist Party. I the only "dressed" woman there, the only not too dreadfully plain. Miss Emily Hobhouse was the Pacifist Beauty. A Kensington curate & his sister sat next me. Max Henckel played.

Sat., Nov. 17. Lunched with Rebecca & Sir Henry Wood.[128] A man took me to the Queen's Hall Concert.

Sun., Nov. 18. Supped in Studio, Stella, taking piece of beef. On to Playfair's.[129]

Mon., Nov. 19. Lunched Von Hutten. They talked of Ford's rudeness & *grossièreté* with me. Saw Aunt Amy after dinner.

[127] R[obert] B[ontine] Cunninghame Graham (1852-1936), British travel and story writer and historian, was a friend of Ford and Conrad. During World War I he went to South America to buy horses for the British Army. Active in radical politics, he served as the first president of the Scottish Labour Party (1888) and in 1928 became the first president of the Scottish National Party.

[128] Sir Henry Wood (1869-1944), British conductor and composer, was known for the Promenade Concert series at Queen's Hall.

[129] Sir Nigel Playfair (1874-1934) acted in Shaw's plays and later became manager of the Lyric Theatre, Hammersmith, famous for its productions of Gay, Congreve, and Wilde.

Tues., Nov. 20. To Marley's. Saw Boothes. Byles dined.

Wed., Nov. 21. The Party without Ford. How will it be? It was all right. 20 of my guests, 20 of theirs. [VH: Stella & Phillis's studio].

Thurs., Nov. 22. I am only thinking of finishing the novel.[130]

Wed., Nov. 28. How badly I keep this. I am wondering what to say to Ford all the time.

Thurs., Nov. 29. To theatre with the Playfairs. Still wondering

Fri., Nov. 30. Dined Scott James.

Sat., Dec. 1. Byles dined

Sun., Dec. 2. Byles lunched. Defries coming & met an authoress Miss Clemence Dane[131] & Mary Butts[132] at the Reid-Bowen ménage. Still what to say to Ford? I want him but am too proud—to receive him on his casual request.

Tues., Dec. 4. Still wondering. I shall call Ford Kühleborn for he is like Undine's Uncle, who when the Knight struck at him dissolved into foam.[133] F is like him. One can neither depend on him or fight him.

Then I come home & find a lyric he has sent me that if it was written to her, any woman would forgive a man anything! [VH: To Stella]

Mon., Dec. 17. Poor Ford's birthday. I sent him a box of preserved fruits & some vests & plants & tablecloths. He sends lovely poems one last prayer but disclaims them saying they are written to *bouts rimés*.

Tues., Dec. 18. Another raid suddenly at 7:30,[134] just as I got in. No warning.

130 Probably *Their Lives*, published in 1918.

131 Clemence Dane (1888-1965), English novelist and dramatist, was born Winifred Ashton. Her first novel, *Regiment of Women*, was published in 1917. She was at various times in her life a portrait painter, a teacher, an actress, and an enthusiastic war worker.

132 Mary Butts (1893-1937) was separated from the poet and publisher John Rodker. She wrote poems and short stories and was active in bohemian society during the twenties.

133 Kühleborn is Undine's uncle in Fouqué's story, a powerful water spirit who often appears in the guise of a river out of which a figure of a man emerges and dissolves. He is tricky and so unstable in form that the knight Huldbrand cannot fight him. Hunt here transforms Ford from male Undine, a more harmless spirit (see entry of July 12), to the powerful and elusive Kühleborn.

134 The following morning the *Times* reported that there had been an evening air raid,

Sun., Dec. 30.   No good this book. But today I saw my sister Silvia & had some sort of reconciliation with her. And Ford has sent me an invitation to a ball at Redcar New Year Eve.

Xmas alone at Soskice's for dinner

New Years Eve to Defries. Danced

Sat., Jan. 19.   F wrote & said "I suppose then our relations are at an end. I am very sorry, but I suppose it had to be." I answered later I am very sorry too

Sun., Jan. 20.   He wrote, If you sorry & I sorry cannot we come together?—Insincere, vain, but a great concession for him. His mother says so. But why need he make concessions. If he isn't ravenous for me, then there is no need to try & come together.

Mon., Jan. 21.   Arranged to go to sleep at Mrs H[ueffer]'s. [VH: his mother].

Tues., Jan. 22.   To Dummett & Alvarez concert & Miss Ashworth. Ford can't come—all leave stopped: *he says*. Still I go to Mrs H's.

Thurs., Jan. 24.   F came—& stayed a week at S Lodge. I stayed at Brook Green[135] but was otherwise friends . . . . He left perfectly pleased with himself, annoyed with me & rather slavish. The test . . . that he was willing to accept board & lodging without me—has worked out. It makes him contemptible.

He said "De Lorge[136]—the man who was sent into the lion's den by the lady for her glove. He got her glove, but never forgave!"

F never forgave me for going to Mrs H's while he was on leave. That did it, finally. [VH: Did it? It was Stella . . . the new passion]

---

with hostile planes crossing the Kent and Essex coasts about 6:15 p.m. and proceeding toward London. Bombs were dropped in Kent, Essex, and the London district.

135 Brook Green was the home of Ford's mother.

136 De Lorge is the hero of a legend found in Froissart and versified by many poets, including Schiller, Bulwer, Leigh Hunt, and Browning. De Lorge's lady dared him to recover her glove that she had tossed into an arena of wild beasts as a test of his love. He accepted the challenge, but on his return flung the glove into her face, his love turned to contempt at this revelation of the lady's character. Ford actually failed Hunt's test of character and fidelity, but like De Lorge he never forgave her for challenging him.